REVISE AQA GCSE
English Language
REVISION WORKBOOK

Series Consultant: Harry Smith

Authors: Jonathan Morgan, Julie Hughes and David Grant

Reviewer: David Grant

Also available to support your revision:

Revise GCSE Study Skills Guide   9781447967071

The **Revise GCSE Study Skills Guide** is full of tried-and-trusted hints and tips for how to learn more effectively. It gives you techniques to help you achieve your best – throughout your GCSE studies and beyond!

Revise GCSE Revision Planner   9781447967828

The **Revise GCSE Revision Planner** helps you to plan and organise your time, step-by-step, throughout your GCSE revision. Use this book and wall chart to mastermind your revision.

For the full range of Pearson revision titles across KS2, KS3, GCSE, Functional Skills, AS/A Level and BTEC visit:
www.pearsonschools.co.uk/revise

Contents

SECTION A: READING

1   The exam papers explained
2   Planning your exam time
3   Paper 1 Reading questions 1
4   Paper 1 Reading questions 2
5   Paper 2 Reading questions 1
6   Paper 2 Reading questions 2
7   Skimming for the main idea
8   Annotating the sources
9   Putting it into practice
10 Putting it into practice
11 The writer's viewpoint
12 Fact, opinion and expert evidence
13 Explicit information and ideas
14 Implicit information and ideas
15 Inference
16 Point–Evidence–Explain
17 Putting it into practice
18 Putting it into practice
19 Word classes
20 Connotations
21 Figurative language
22 Creation of character
23 Creating atmosphere
24 Narrative voice
25 Putting it into practice
26 Putting it into practice
27 Rhetorical devices 1
28 Rhetorical devices 2
29 Whole text structure: fiction
30 Whole text structure: non-fiction
31 Identifying sentence types
32 Commenting on sentences
33 Putting it into practice
34 Putting it into practice
35 Evaluating a fiction text 1
36 Evaluating a fiction text 2
37 Using evidence to evaluate
38 Putting it into practice
39 Writing about two texts
40 Selecting evidence for synthesis
41 Answering a synthesis question
42 Looking closely at language
43 Planning to compare language
44 Comparing language
45 Comparing structure
46 Comparing ideas
47 Comparing perspective
48 Answering a comparison question
49 Putting it into practice

SECTION B: WRITING

50 Writing questions: an overview
51 Writing questions: Paper 1
52 Writing questions: Paper 2
53 Writing questions: time management
54 Writing for a purpose: creative 1
55 Writing for a purpose: creative 2
56 Writing for a purpose: viewpoint 1
57 Writing for a purpose: viewpoint 2
58 Writing for an audience
59 Putting it into practice

60 Putting it into practice
61 Form: articles
62 Form: letters and reports
63 Form: speeches
64 Putting it into practice
65 Ideas and planning: creative
66 Structure: creative
67 Beginnings and endings: creative
68 Putting it into practice
69 Ideas and planning: viewpoint 1
70 Ideas and planning: viewpoint 2
71 Openings: viewpoint
72 Conclusions: viewpoint
73 Putting it into practice
74 Paragraphing
75 Linking ideas
76 Putting it into practice
77 Formality and standard English 1
78 Formality and standard English 2
79 Vocabulary for effect: synonyms
80 Vocabulary for effect: creative
81 Vocabulary for effect: viewpoint
82 Language for different effects 1
83 Language for different effects 2
84 Language for different effects 3
85 Putting it into practice
86 Putting it into practice
87 Sentence variety 1
88 Sentence variety 2
89 Sentences for different effects
90 Putting it into practice
91 Ending a sentence
92 Commas
93 Apostrophes and speech punctuation
94 Colons, semi-colons, dashes, brackets and ellipses
95 Putting it into practice
96 Common spelling errors 1
97 Common spelling errors 2
98 Common spelling errors 3
99 Proofreading
100 Putting it into practice
101 Source 8 – *One Day in the Life of Ivan Denisovich*
102 Source 9 – *Enduring Love*
103 Source 10 – *To Kill a Mockingbird*
104 Source 11 – *The Day of the Triffids*
105 Source 12a – 'Occupations Accessible to Women: Elementary Teaching'
106 Source 12b – 'OK, you try teaching 13-year-olds'
107 Source 13a – *The Boys Are Back in Town*
108 Source 13b – 'The Rearing and Management of Children: Moral Influence – Obedience'
109 Source 14a – ''Appy ever after'
110 Source 14b – 'Victorian Hypnotism'

111 PRACTICE PAPERS

121 ANSWERS

. . . .
A small bit of small print
AQA publishes Sample Assessment Material and the Specification on its website. This is the official content and this book should be used in conjunction with it. The questions in *Now try this* have been written to help you practise every topic in the book. Remember: the real exam questions may not look like this.

The exam papers explained

The English Language GCSE is split into two exam papers:
- Paper 1: Explorations in creative reading and writing
- Paper 2: Writers' viewpoints and perspectives

Each paper has a reading section (Section A) and a writing section (Section B).
Remind yourself of the content of each exam then answer the questions that follow:

Paper 1, Section A: Reading
You will be asked to read one fiction text from the 20th or 21st century that will be approximately 500–800 words long. You will be asked four questions that will test your understanding of the text.

Paper 1, Section B: Writing
You will be asked to write a descriptive or narrative piece of writing from a choice of two. One of the questions will have a visual stimulus to help you generate ideas.

how do you get higher marks in!
tls Rees?

For each paper, you are advised to spend 15 minutes at the start reading through the sources and questions. If you read the questions first then you can make notes as you read the sources. You should also leave time to check through your answers at the end.

Paper 2, Section A: Reading
You will be asked to read one non-fiction text and one non-literary text – these will be drawn from the 19th century, and either the 20th or 21st century. You will be asked four questions that will test your understanding of the text.

Paper 2, Section B: Writing
You will be asked to write a text for a particular target audience on a theme that will have been introduced in the reading section.

1 (a) Which paper asks you to read a 19th century non-fiction or non-literary text? ....

   (b) Which paper (and section) asks you to use a visual stimulus? ....

   (c) What are you advised to do for 15 minutes at the start of each exam? ....

   (d) Do you have a choice for any of the questions? If so, which one? ....

   (e) How many questions in total will you be asked to complete for each exam? ....

   (f) What should you leave time for before the end of each exam? ....

As well as ensuring that you revise thoroughly, it is also vital that you plan effectively for the exam day itself by ensuring that you are physically and mentally prepared.

2 Read the following advice and decide whether you think it is good advice (tick) or bad advice (cross).
   A Have plenty of caffeine before the exam.   ☐
   B Make sure that you include everything you have revised.   ☐
   C Hydrate yourself – bring water to the exam.   ☐
   D Breathe quickly during the exam to help with speed.   ☐
   E Make sure you write constantly for the whole exam.   ☐
   F Make sure your writing is legible.   ☐

You can't predict what the source material will be, nor can you guess what the writing question will be on; however, it is possible to revise the text types to develop your wider reading and writing skills.

3 Complete the table with some examples of the types of reading and writing you have done or still need to do.

	Title	Genre	Audience	Purpose
Non-fiction				
Fiction				

1

Planning your exam time

Time management is a vital part of being successful in your exams. Using the reading time effectively, and allocating the correct amount of time per question, will enable you to show off your skills and maximise your chances of getting the result that you deserve.

1 Use your 15 minutes reading time at the start of the exam productively. Put the following statements in the order you think will be helpful. Number them from 1 to 5 with 1 being the task you do first:

A Skim read the sources so you know roughly the main themes. ☐

B Annotate the sources with brief notes that relate to the questions. ☐

C Read the sources – especially the introductory information as it will provide you with important clues about the genre, form, purpose and target audience. ☐

D Read the questions before you read the sources so you know what to look for. ☐

E Ensure you have highlighter pens to pick out different features (though don't highlight indiscriminately – only parts that are relevant to the questions set!). ☐

> Work out how long you should spend on each question according to the number of marks it is worth, e.g. a 4-mark question should take approximately 4 minutes to complete.

2 Complete the table below by working out how much time you could spend on each question.

Paper 1		Marks allocated	Time I should spend
	Reading time		15 minutes
Section A: Reading	Q1	4	
	Q2	8	
	Q3	8	
	Q4	20	
Section B: Writing	Planning time		5 minutes
	Q5	40	
	Checking my answers		5 minutes
	Total time:		1 hour and 45 minutes

Paper 2		Marks allocated	Time I should spend
	Reading time		15 minutes
Section A: Reading	Q1	4	
	Q2	8	
	Q3	12	
	Q4	16	
Section B: Writing	Planning time		5 minutes
	Q5	40	
	Checking my answers		5 minutes
	Total time:		1 hour and 45 minutes

Paper 1 Reading questions 1

It is important that you understand how each question is being assessed. The examiner will have a specific mark scheme that will be used to decide on the mark for your answer.

In **Paper 1, Section A: Reading Question 1**, you are assessed for:

> **Assessment objective 1**
> (a) Identify and interpret explicit and implicit information and ideas
> (b) Select and synthesise evidence from different texts

1 Read the exam-style question below. **You don't need to answer it**. Instead, identify which part of assessment objective 1 the question tests. Circle your choice.

Paper
1

> **1.** Read again the first part of source 10, **lines 1 to 20**.
> List **four** reasons why the children dislike visiting
> Mrs Dubose. **(4 marks)**

> Question 1 will direct you to a specific part of the source and ask you to select specific information – there is no need for a detailed analysis.

This question tests: AO1(a)   AO1(b)

In **Paper 1, Section A: Reading Question 2**, you are assessed for:

> **Assessment objective 2**
> Explain, comment on and analyse how writers use language and structure to achieve effects and influence readers, using relevant subject terminology to support their views

2 Read the exam-style question below. **You don't need to answer it**.

Paper
1

> **2.** Look in detail at this extract from **lines 22 to 32** of the source.
> How does the writer use language here to reveal the children's fear of Mrs Dubose?
> You could include the writer's choice of:
> • words and phrases
> • language features and techniques
> • sentence forms. **(8 marks)**

> Question 2 will direct you to a specific part of the source and ask you for a longer answer that refers to the way a writer uses **language** to create particular effects.

(a) Circle the key information in the question.

(b) How long should you spend on this question? ....

3 Which assessment focus would you expect the following exam-style questions to be assessed on? Circle your choice.

(a)

> How does the writer use language to help generate excitement in the text?

AO1(a)   AO1(b)   AO2

(b)

> Identify four aspects of Mrs Dubose's character.

AO1(a)   AO1(b)   AO2

Paper 1 Reading questions 2

For Question 3 and Question 4 in **Paper 1, Section A: Reading**, it is important that you produce a developed, analytical response that reveals your understanding of the writer at work.

In **Paper 1, Section A: Reading Question 3**, you are assessed for:

Assessment objective 2
Explain, comment on and analyse how writers use language and structure to achieve effects and influence readers, using relevant subject terminology to support their views

Read the exam-style question below. **You don't need to answer it**.

Paper ①

3. You now need to think about the **whole** of the **source**.
   This text is taken from the opening of a novel.
   How has the writer structured the text to interest you as a reader?
   You could write about:
   • what the writer focuses your attention on at the beginning
   • how and why the writer changes this focus as the extract develops
   • any other structural features that interest you.   **(8 marks)**

> Question 3 will ask you to refer to the whole of the source and comment on how the writer has used **structure** to create particular effects on the reader.

1 Tick the statements that you think apply to the question:
   A   I need to look at a specific section from the source.   ☐
   B   I don't need to use evidence to support my analysis.   ☐
   C   I should comment on language and structure.   ☐
   D   I should spend approximately 8 minutes on this question.   ☐
   E   I should refer to the writer at work.   ☐
   F   I need to use comparison skills to answer this question.   ☐
   G   I need to consider the impact of the text on the reader.   ☐

In **Paper 1, Section A: Reading Question 4**, you are assessed for:

Assessment objective 4
Evaluate texts critically and support this with appropriate textual references

> Question 4 will ask you to refer to a particular section from the source and assesses your ability to evaluate the impact of the text on the reader. You are also encouraged to provide a personal response to the question, using textual evidence to support your analysis.

Read the exam-style question below. **You don't need to answer it**.

Paper ①

4. Focus this part of your answer on the second half of the source, **from lines 29 to 51**.
   A student, having read this section of the text said: "The narrator doesn't seem to take any responsibility for what happened."
   To what extent do you agree? In your response, you could:
   • write about your own impression of the narrator's involvement in the incident
   • evaluate how the writer presents the narrator's involvement
   • support your opinions with quotations from the text.   **(20 marks)**

2 Tick the statements that you think apply to this question:
   A   My personal opinion is not allowed.   ☐
   B   I need to use evidence to support my analysis.   ☐
   C   I should refer to the whole of the source.   ☐
   D   I should refer to a specific section of the source.   ☐
   E   I should spend 20 minutes on the question.   ☐
   F   I need to evaluate the text critically.   ☐

Paper 2 Reading questions 1

There are a variety of question types in Paper 2, which also include a comparison of texts.

In **Paper 2, Section A: Reading Questions 1 and 2**, you are assessed for:

Assessment objective 1
(a) Identify and interpret explicit and implicit information and ideas
(b) Select and synthesise evidence from different texts

In Question 1, you will be directed to a specific part of the source and there will be some true and false statements listed. It is important that you carefully consider each possible statement and only shade the number of boxes you have been asked to shade.

Read the exam-style questions below. **You do not need to answer them.** Then answer the questions at the bottom of the page.

Question 1 has been completed by a student.

Paper ② 1. Read again **source 13b, lines 1 to 7**.
Choose **four** statements below which are TRUE.
- Shade the boxes of the ones that you think are true.
- Choose a maximum of four statements.
  A People are deluded if they think no harm can come to a child if they get their own way. ■
  B Babies should get their own way until they are older. ☐
  C Babies are easy to manage. ☐
  D Children should be taught obedience. ■
  E Rules are there to be broken. ☐
  F Obedience is the first lesson to be taught. ■
  G Rules are not important to babies. ☐
  H Well-managed babies understand the meaning of obedience. ☐

(4 marks)

In Question 2 you will be asked to refer to two sources and you select relevant evidence from both sources to support your ideas.

Paper ② 2. You need to refer to **source 12a** and **source 12b** for this question.
Use details from **both** sources.
Write a summary of how both writers present the teaching profession. (8 marks)

1 (a) Which question is asking you to make links between two texts? ....

  (b) How long should you spend on Question 1? ....

  (c) How long should you spend on Question 2? ....

  (d) Which question is asking you to focus on a part of the source? ....

  (e) How do you show your answer to Question 1? ....

  (f) Where has the student gone wrong in answering Question 1? ....

  (g) Which question is asking you to synthesise? ....

'Synthesise' means 'summarise'.

Paper 2 Reading questions 2

In **Paper 2, Section A: Reading Question 3**, you are assessed for:

Assessment objective 2
Explain, comment on and analyse how writers use language and structure to achieve effects and influence readers, using relevant subject terminology to support their views

1 Read the exam-style question below. **You don't need to answer it**. Instead, annotate the question to show the following information:
- how many texts you need to refer to
- how much of the text you need to use
- which are the key words
- how long to spend on writing an answer.

> You will be asked a question on the 19th-century source and will be expected to refer to the whole of the extract.

Paper

> 3. You now need to refer **only** to **source 13b**.
> How does the writer use language to express her viewpoints on parenting?　　**(12 marks)**

In **Paper 2, Section A: Reading Question 4**, you are assessed for:

Assessment objective 3
Compare writers' ideas and perspectives, as well as how they are conveyed, across two or more texts

2 (a) Read the exam-style question below. The table shows one student's planning for the question where they have found evidence for each of the bullet points. Write the bullet points in the correct place in column 1 of the table.

Paper

> 4. For this question, you need to refer to the **whole of source 13a** together with **source 13b**.
> Compare how the two writers convey their different attitudes towards children.
> In your answer, you could:
> - compare their different attitudes
> - compare the methods they use to convey their attitudes
> - support your ideas with quotations from both texts.　　**(16 marks)**

In your answer, you could:	**13a** *The Boys are Back in Town* (21st century)	**13b** *Cassell's Household Guide* (19th century)
	The fact is, I run a pretty loose ship	Obedience is the first lesson to be taught
	Laid back and relaxed	Strict and uncompromising
	Colloquial language	Use of imperatives

(b) Annotate the exam-style Question 4 in the same way as you did for exam-style Question 3 above, using the bullet points listed in Question 1.

Skimming for the main idea

Look at this short extract from source 12b on page 106, 'OK, you try teaching 13-year-olds', then answer the questions below.

21st

OK, you try teaching 13-year-olds

Shocking news: a young trainee languages teacher on placement at Tarleton High in Lancashire "lost it" in class, barricaded the door with furniture, trapping the pupils, and threatened to kill them with something nasty that she had in her handbag.

Guided **1** What does the headline suggest about the main idea or theme of the article?

The headline suggests that the main idea of the article will be the difficulties faced by teachers.

Guided **2** What does the opening sentence suggest about the main idea or theme of the article?

The opening sentence suggests that the main idea will be the difficulties of teaching, although it

also suggests ....

....

....

Now read these sentences from the end of the same article, then answer the questions below.

21st

Her career is now ruined. But the children were "petrified ... burst into tears" and were offered "support". The pathetic little wets. She was pretending, you fools – dredging up a last desperate ploy to shut the monsters up. If she had cried, they would have laughed out loud. Hopefully, she won't be sacked. If that's what she really, really wants.

3 What does the end suggest about the article's main idea or theme?

....

....

4 Do the ideas expressed at the end of the article differ from those you found at the beginning?

....

....

> Skim reading a text can give you a good idea of what it is about before you read it more closely. Look at:
> • the headline, title or headings
> • the first sentence of each paragraph
> • the last sentence of the text.

Turn to the full article, 'OK, you try teaching 13-year-olds', on page 106.
Skim read it for 30 seconds, then answer Question 5.

5 In one sentence, sum up the main idea in the article as a whole.

....

....

....

Annotating the sources

Read this short annotated extract from *The Day of the Triffids* on page 104. It has been annotated by a student.

20th

> It would have been almost spherical but for three bluntly-tapered projections extending from the lower part. Supported on these, the main body was lifted <u>about a foot clear of the ground.</u>
>
> When it 'walked' it moved <u>rather like a man on crutches.</u> Two of the blunt 'legs' slid forward, then <u>the whole thing lurched</u> as the rear one drew almost level with them, then the two in front slid forward again. At each 'step' the long stem <u>whipped violently back and forth;</u> it gave one a kind of seasick feeling to watch it. As a method of progress it looked both strenuous and <u>clumsy</u> – faintly reminiscent of <u>young elephants at play.</u>

A   Simile – sense of the familiar

B   Verb and adverb choice reinforces sense of unpredictability and physical danger

C   Makes it sound endearing

D   Out of control and clumsy movement, potentially dangerous

E   Not very big

Now read this exam-style question. **You don't need to answer it.** Instead, think about what it is asking you to do, then answer the questions that follow.

Paper 1

2. Look in detail at **lines 35 to 38** of the source on page 104.

How does the writer use language here to make the triffids seem both strange and threatening?

You could include the writer's choice of:

- words and phrases
- language features and techniques
- sentence forms. **(8 marks)**

Guided

1 Which of the annotations A to E above would help you to answer Question 2? Circle your choices.

2 Why won't annotation detail E help you to answer Question 2?

....

....

Now read the rest of source 11, *The Day of the Triffids* on page 104 then answer Question 3.

3 Annotate the extract from *The Day of the Triffids* on page 104, identifying any words or phrases that would help you to answer the exam-style question below. **You don't need to answer the exam-style question itself**.

Paper 1

4. Focus this part of your answer on the second half of the source, **from line 35 to the end**.

A student, having read this section of the text said: "In the last twenty lines or so of this passage, the writer increases the tension as it finally becomes clear that the triffids are dangerous."

To what extent do you agree?

In your response, you could:

- write about your own impressions of the tension and the way it is increased
- evaluate how the writer has created these impressions
- support your opinions with quotations from the text. **(20 marks)**

Putting it into practice

Read the full extract from *Enduring Love* in source 9 on page 102, then answer Questions 1 and 2 below.

1 (a) Highlight, circle or underline any words or phrases in the extract from *Enduring Love* that would help you to answer the exam-style question below.

Paper
①

2. Look in detail at **lines 14 to 21** of the source.

How does the writer use language here effectively to describe the rescue?

You could include the writer's choice of:

• words and phrases

• language features and techniques

• sentence forms.   **(8 marks)**

(b) Make notes about the effect that each word or phrase you have identified has on the reader.

....

....

....

....

....

....

2 Now use your annotations and notes from Question 1 to write the first two paragraphs of an answer to the exam-style Question 2.

> When you tackle this kind of question in the exam, remember to:
> • spend about 8 minutes on your answer
> • highlight key words in the question so that you get the focus right
> • use only the lines of the text referred to in the question.

....

....

....

....

....

....

....

....

....

....

....

....

....

....

Remember: You are only being asked to write part of an answer on this page. In the exam, you will be given more space to write a full answer.

Had a go ☐   Nearly there ☐   Nailed it! ☐

Putting it into practice

Read the full extract from 'The Rearing and Management of Children', in source 13b on page 108, then answer Questions 1 and 2 below.

1 (a) Highlight, circle or underline any words or phrases in the extract that would help you to answer the exam-style question below.

Paper
②

3. You now need to refer **only** to **source 13b**.

How does the writer use language to present their opinions of children?   **(12 marks)**

(b) Make notes about the effect that each word or phrase you have identified has on the reader.

....

....

....

....

....

....

....

2 Now use your annotations and notes from Question 1 to write the first two paragraphs of an answer to the exam-style Question 3.

> When you tackle this kind of question in the exam, remember to:
> • spend about 12 minutes on your answer
> • highlight key words in the question so that you get the focus right
> • focus on the way the ideas and point of view are expressed by the writer.

....

....

....

....

....

....

....

....

....

....

....

....

....

> **Remember:** You are only being asked to write part of an answer on this page. In the exam, you will be given more space to write a full answer.

The writer's viewpoint

Being able quickly to establish the viewpoint of the writer is vital to developing a secure understanding of the reading texts for Paper 2.

In the table below are extracts from the source materials for Paper 2 that can be found on pages 101–110.

Guided Complete the table by briefly indicating what you think the writer's viewpoint is on the topic they are discussing. Some examples have been completed for you.

Topic		Writer's viewpoint		Writer's viewpoint
Education	**Source 12a** Some hard study would, in some cases, be needed to supply the inaccuracy of the general style of a woman's knowledge…	Sexist attitude towards women, suggesting they are inferior and less intelligent.	**Source 12b** I blame the parents, partly. They often think teacher is a child-minding serf and their huge babies are innocent and truthful. A big mistake.	The writer is sympathetic towards the problems teachers face and is clearly placing the responsibility on parents – revealed by the mocking tone deployed.
Parenting	**Source 13a** But essentially, here was only one rule: they had to do what I told them. The advantage of this regime was obvious to them: I told them less – much less – than half of what two parents would tell them to do.	....	**Source 13b** If children were left to their own choice, they would be eating and drinking perpetually of whatever came in their way, till the stomach could no longer retain the improper substances.	....
Power of the mind	**Source 14a** You mean hack my brain to make me feel what I want to feel, rather than what I actually feel? I ask.	....	**Source 14b** He may even be transformed into a beast, or an inanimate thing like a chair or a carpet, and in every case will act out all the details of the part with a sincerity and intensity seldom seen at the theatre.	....

Fact, opinion and expert evidence

Read the following three quotations from an article about teaching, then answer Question 1.

A In 2013, almost 50,000 teachers gave up teaching.

B Research from the Department for Education suggests that difficult working conditions are the main cause.

C Teaching is the most rewarding of all professions.

1 Identify which of the above extracts is:

(a) a fact ....

(b) an opinion ....

(c) expert evidence ....

> Think about how the fact, opinion or expert evidence helps to support the writer's viewpoint or argument.

Now read the short extract from source 12b 'OK, you try teaching 13-year-olds' below. Then answer Questions 2 to 4.

21st

> I'm trying not to sound bitter here, but I have taught; I have known supply-teaching hell; and I, too, have blown my top, even though it was 3.30pm and nearly over, because by then they were still climbing up walls (really), throwing scissors, dribbling glue and screaming all the while … and when that happens, sometimes one just cannot keep one's cool a second longer.
>
> And 13 is a particularly cruel age. In my first year's teaching, I crashed the car and sliced my forehead open on the sun-visor. Back at school, with my unsightly 27-stitch scar, I passed two 13-year-old girls. "She looks uglier than ever," said they, laughing merrily.

2 Write one sentence summing up the writer's viewpoint in the extract above.

....

....

3 Identify at least one fact, one opinion and one piece of expert evidence the writer uses to support her viewpoint. Highlight or underline these in the extract above.

4 Write a sentence for each example you have identified in Question 3, explaining how it supports the writer's viewpoint.

> Remember that the person providing the expert evidence could be the writer of the text, as in this case!

Fact: ....

....

Opinion: ....

....

Expert evidence: ....

....

Explicit information and ideas

Read lines 10–23 from source 8 on page 101, *One Day in the Life of Ivan Denisovich*, then look at the exam-style question below. **You don't need to answer this question**. Instead, think about what it is asking you to do, and how this student has highlighted the relevant sections and stated the four possible answers.

> There is no need for a detailed explanation or analysis of language – you just simply need to identify the correct answers.

 Paper ①

Read again the first part of the source, **lines 1 to 3**.

1. List **four** things from this part of the text that we learn from Shukhov. **(4 marks)**

A. He never overslept.

B. He was good at stitch work.

C. He made money on the side.

D. He didn't forget what his team-leader had told him.

Now read lines 1–9 from source 9, *Enduring Love*, on page 102, and answer the exam-style question below.

 20th

> What we saw when we stood from our picnic was this: a huge grey balloon, the size of a house, the shape of a teardrop, had come down in the field. The pilot must have been halfway out of the passenger basket as it touched the ground. His leg had become entangled in a rope that was attached to an anchor. Now, as the wind gusted and pushed and lifted the balloon toward the escarpment, he was being half dragged, half carried across the field. In the basket was a child, a boy of about ten. In a sudden lull, the man was on his feet, clutching at the basket, or at the boy. Then there was another gust, and the pilot was on his back, bumping over the rough ground, trying to dig his feet in for purchase or lunging for the anchor behind him in order to secure it in the earth. Even if he had been able, he would not have dared disentangle himself from the anchor rope. He needed his weight to keep the balloon on the ground, and the wind could have snatched the rope from his hands.

 Paper ①

1. Read again the first part of the source, **lines 1 to 9**.

List **four** things from this part of the text that we discover about the man in the balloon. **(4 marks)**

(a) ....

(b) ....

(c) ....

(d) ....

> For this type of question, keep your answers as short as possible. Don't copy whole sentences from the source in your answers.

Implicit information and ideas

Read this short extract from *One Day in the Life of Ivan Denisovich*:

As usual, at five o'clock that morning reveille was sounded by the blows of a hammer on a length of rail hanging up near the staff quarters. The intermittent sounds barely penetrated the window-panes on which the frost lay two fingers thick and then ended almost as soon as they'd begun. It was cold outside, and the camp-guard was reluctant to go on beating out the reveille for long.

The clanging ceased, but everything outside still looked like the middle of the night when Ivan Denisovich Shukhov got up to go to the bucket. It was pitch dark except for the yellow light cast on the window by three lamps – two in the outer zone, one inside the camp itself.

Now look at this exam-style question relating to the text extract. **You don't need to answer it**. Instead, answer Question 1 below.

Paper

1. Read again the first part of the source, **lines 1 to 7**.
   List **four** reasons from this part of the text why the labour camp is an unpleasant place.   **(4 marks)**

> To identify implicit ideas you need to read between the lines and think about what the writer is suggesting or implying. Explicit ideas are not hidden – you just need to find short quotations or paraphrase what is already in the text.

Guided   1   Read one student's answer to exam-style Question 1. For each point, decide whether the information is explicit or implicit.

The hammer is used to wake them up.	(Explicit) / Implicit
They have to get up at five o'clock.	Explicit / Implicit
The windows are covered with thick frost.	(Explicit) / Implicit
The sun is not yet up.	Explicit / Implicit

Now read this extract, also from *One Day in the Life of Ivan Denisovich*, then answer Question 2.

He didn't get up. He lay there in his bunk on the top tier, his head buried in a blanket and a coat, his two feet stuffed into one sleeve, with the end tucked under, of his wadded jacket. He couldn't see, but his ears told him everything going on in the barrack-room and especially in the corner his team occupied. He heard the heavy tread of the orderlies carrying one of the big barrels of nightsoil along the passage outside. A light job, that was considered, a job for the infirm, but just you try and carry out the muck without spilling any. He heard some of the 75th slamming bunches of boots on to the floor from the drying-shed. Now their own lads were doing it (it was their own team's turn, too, to dry valenki). Tiurin, the team-leader, and his deputy Pavlo put on their valenki, without a word but he heard their bunks creaking.

2   Find four implicit ideas in the extract above that suggest that life in the labour camp is unpleasant.

(a) ....

(b) ....

(c) ....

(d) ....

> Short questions on explicit and implicit information are only worth one mark for each point you make, so keep your answers brief. You don't always need to use quotations – you can also use your own words.

Inference

Read this short extract from source 10, *To Kill a Mockingbird*, then answer Questions 1 and 2 below. Full text on page 103.

> I didn't look any more than I had to. Jem re-opened *Ivanhoe* and began reading. I tried to keep up with him, but he read too fast. When Jem came to a word he didn't know, he skipped it, but Mrs Dubose would catch him and make him spell it out. Jem read for perhaps twenty minutes, during which time I looked at the soot-stained mantelpiece, out of the window, anywhere to keep from looking at her.

1 Highlight or underline any phrases in the extract above that suggest the children dislike Mrs Dubose.

Guided

2 What impression of Mrs Dubose do you get from this short extract? Include two points, and use a short quotation to support each point and back up your answer.

> When answering a question like this, think about what is suggested or implied about a character by the actions of other characters in the scene.

   (a) The extract suggests that Mrs Dubose is ....

   ....

   ....

   (b) ....

   ....

Now read this short extract, also from source 10, *To Kill a Mockingbird*, then answer Question 3 below.

> The following Monday afternoon Jem and I climbed the steep front steps to Mrs Dubose's house and padded down the open hallway. Jem, armed with Ivanhoe and full of superior knowledge, knocked at the second door on the left.
>
> 'Mrs Dubose?' he called.
>
> Jessie opened the wood door and unlatched the screen door.
>
> 'Is that you, Jem Finch?' she said. 'You got your sister with you. I don't know –'
>
> 'Let 'em both in, Jessie,' said Mrs Dubose. Jessie admitted us and went off to the kitchen.
>
> An oppressive odour met us when we crossed the threshold, an odour I had met many times in rain-rotted grey houses where there are coal-oil lamps, water diggers, and unbleached domestic sheets. It always made me afraid, expectant, watchful.
>
> In the corner of the room was a brass bed, and in the bed was Mrs Dubose. I wondered if Jem's activities had put her there, and for a moment I felt quite sorry for her. She was lying under a pile of quilts and looked almost friendly.
>
> There was a marble-topped washstand by her bed; on it were a glass with a teaspoon in it, a red ear syringe, a box of absorbent cotton, and a steel alarm clock standing on three tiny legs.
>
> 'So you brought that dirty little sister of yours, did you?' was her greeting.
>
> Jem said quietly, 'My sister ain't dirty and I ain't scared of you,' although I noticed his knees were shaking.

Guided

3 Write about your impressions of Mrs Dubose and her house.

> Mrs Dubose's house seems intimidating from the start of the extract, as it has 'steep front steps'. The house also frightens the children as they are met by an 'oppressive odour', which makes the narrator 'afraid, expectant' and 'watchful'. The odour is described as something usually smelt in 'rain-rotted' houses, which gives the reader the impression that the house

....

....

....

Point–Evidence–Explain

Read this short extract from source 12b, 'OK, you try teaching 13-year-olds', then answer the questions that follow.

> Shocking news: a young trainee languages teacher on placement at Tarleton High in Lancashire "lost it" in class, barricaded the door with furniture, trapping the pupils, and threatened to kill them with something nasty that she had in her handbag. But why shocking? Imagine yourself in her place, "teaching" about 30 13- or 14-year-old creatures. Do you have one or two in your house? Are they polite, quiet and cooperative? Or are they breathtakingly insolent, noisy, crabby, offensive, skulking, smoking, drugging, and whingeing that they are not suitably entertained? What if you had 30? Wouldn't you like something in your handbag to shut the little toads up?

1 The point below could be used to comment on the writer's use of language and its effect on the reader. Which piece of evidence below (A or B) most effectively supports this point? Circle your choice.

> **Point:** The writer uses lists of adjectives to emphasise how difficult it can be to deal with teenagers.
>
> **Evidence A:** 'whingeing that they are not suitably entertained'
>
> **Evidence B:** 'insolent, noisy, crabby, offensive, …'

2 Explain why the evidence you have chosen is the most effective for supporting the above point.

....

....

Guided 3 Select effective evidence from the extract to support the point below. Then choose the most effective explanation from the options given. Circle your choice.

> **Point:** The writer uses strong verbs to emphasise the shocking nature of the teacher's actions.
>
> **Evidence:** For example, she uses the words . . . .
>
> . . . .
>
> **Explanation A:** These verbs emphasise how badly the teacher treated the children.
>
> **Explanation B:** These verbs suggest that the teacher treated the children like prisoners. They also give the impression that she had completely lost her ability to manage the class and that she literally wanted to cause them harm.

4 Write one or two sentences, explaining which of the above you think is more effective and why.

....

....

....

> Point–Evidence–Explain, or P-E-E, is particularly useful if you are asked to comment on language and structure, or to evaluate or compare a text. Improve your P-E-E paragraphs by using more than one piece of evidence to support a fully developed point.

Putting it into practice

Read the full extract from *The Day of the Triffids*, in source 11 on page 104, then answer the exam-style question below.

Paper
①

1. Read again the first part of the source, **lines 1 to 5**.
   List **four** reasons from this part of the text why the triffids have not previously been seen as dangerous.   **(4 marks)**

1 (a) ....

  (b) ....

  (c) ....

  (d) ....

2 Now write two P-E-E paragraphs of an answer to the exam-style question below. This question relates to source 11, *The Day of the Triffids* on page 104.

> When you tackle this kind of question in the exam, remember to:
> - spend about 10 minutes on your answer
> - identify the main focus of the question
> - read the text carefully and annotate it with your ideas
> - only use the lines of the extract referred to in the question
> - comment on how the writer uses language and structure and what the effects are on the reader.

Paper
①

2. Look in detail at **lines 19 to 31** of the source.
   How does the writer use language here to reveal the early reactions to the triffids?
   You could include the writer's choice of:
   - words and phrases
   - language features and techniques
   - sentence forms.   **(8 marks)**

....

....

....

....

....

....

....

....

> **Remember:** You are only being asked to write part of an answer on this page. In the exam, where you will write a full answer, you will have more space for your answer.

Had a go ☐   Nearly there ☐   Nailed it! ☐

Putting it into practice

Read the full extract from 'Victorian Hypnotism', in source 14b on page 110. Then write three P-E-E paragraphs of an answer to the exam-style question below.

> When you tackle this kind of question in the exam, remember to:
> · spend about 12 minutes on your answer
> · identify the main focus of the question
> · read the text carefully and annotate it with your ideas
> · comment on how the writer uses language and what the effects are on the reader.

Paper ②

3. You now need to refer **only** to **source 14b**.

How does the writer use language to interest the reader in hypnotism?   **(12 marks)**

....

....

....

....

....

....

....

....

....

....

....

....

....

....

....

....

....

....

....

....

....

....

....

....

> **Remember:** You are only being asked to write part of an answer on this page. In the exam, where you will write a full answer, you will have more space for your writing.

Word classes

Read this short extract from 'OK, you try teaching 13-year-olds', then answer Questions 1 and 2.

> **21st**
>
> Shocking news: a young trainee languages teacher on placement at Tarleton High in Lancashire "lost it" in class, (barricaded) the door with furniture, trapping the pupils, and threatened to kill them with something nasty that she had in her handbag. But why shocking? Imagine yourself in her place, "teaching" about 30 13- or 14-year-old creatures. Do you have one or two in your house? Are they polite, quiet and cooperative? Or are they (breathtakingly) insolent, noisy, crabby, offensive, skulking, smoking, drugging, and whingeing that they are not suitably entertained?

Verb ——

Adverb ——

Guided

1 Circle and label at least one example of each of the following word classes. Two have been done for you:

- noun
- verb
- adverb
- adjective.

> Remember that adjectives can become comparatives (e.g. noisier, more insolent) and superlatives (e.g. noisiest, most insolent).

2 The writer uses lists of adjectives in her rhetorical questions about teenagers. What effect do these lists of adjectives have on the reader?

....

....

....

....

....

Now read this short extract from *One Day in the Life of Ivan Denisovich*, then answer Question 3.

> **20th**
>
> Ah, but not simply to report as usual to the authorities who distributed the daily assignments. Shukhov remembered that this morning his fate hung in the balance: they wanted to shift the 104th from the building-shops to a new site, the 'Socialist Way of Life' settlement. It lay in open country covered with snow-drifts, and before anything else could be done there they would have to dig pits and put up posts and attach barbed wire to them. Wire themselves in, so that they wouldn't run away. Only then would they start building.

3 In this source, the writer uses action verbs to explain his tasks in the labour camp. Identify two examples of action verbs and explain their effects on the reader. Suggest alternative action verbs to emphasise the harshness of life in the camp.

(a) ....

....

....

(b) ....

....

....

Connotations

Read this short extract from source 13a, *The Boys Are Back in Town*, then answer Question 1.

21st

It is what I like to think of as a masculine quality, the theory of (outer markers). The boys have very definite limits that they mustn't go beyond. Inside the (perimeter) they can do very much as they please, but they must stay inside the (boundaries). It's murky on the other side, they're frightened of the dark out there, I've had to see to that. But within the limits it's summertime and it's easy living.

1 (a) Draw lines to match the circled words or phrases to their possible connotations.

(outer markers)   (perimeter)   (boundaries)

border   sport   outer space   outskirts   extreme edge   dividing line   cricket pitch   limits

> Words can have different meanings depending on their context – what comes before and after them in a text. Thinking about the context of a word will help you to understand its connotations.

(b) What ideas and attitudes about parenting do the circled words or phrases suggest to the reader?

....

....

....

Now read this short extract from source 10, *To Kill a Mockingbird*, then answer Question 2.

20th

The following Monday afternoon Jem and I climbed the steep front steps to Mrs Dubose's house and padded down the open hallway. Jem, armed with *Ivanhoe* and full of superior knowledge, knocked at the second door on the left.

'Mrs Dubose?' he called.

Jessie opened the wood door and unlatched the screen door.

'Is that you, Jem Finch?' she said. 'You got your sister with you. I don't know –'

'Let 'em both in, Jessie,' said Mrs Dubose. Jessie admitted us and went off to the kitchen.

An oppressive odour met us when we crossed the threshold, an odour I had met many times in rain-rotted grey houses where there are coal-oil lamps, water dippers, and unbleached domestic sheets.

2 Circle two words or phrases from the source above. Write a sentence commenting on the connotations of each one.

(a)...

....

....

(b)...

....

....

Figurative language

Read this short extract from source 10, *To Kill a Mockingbird*, then answer Question 1. Full text on page 103.

> She was horrible. Her face was the colour of a dirty pillowcase, and the corners of her mouth glistened with wet, which inched like a glacier down the deep grooves enclosing her chin. Old-age liver spots dotted her cheeks and her pale eyes had black pinpoint pupils. Her hands were knobby, and the cuticles were grown up over her fingernails. Her bottom plate was not in, and her upper lip protruded; from time to time she would draw her nether lip to her upper plate and carry her chin with it. This made the wet move faster.

Guided ⟩

1 The writer uses the word 'glacier' figuratively. What does this simile suggest to the reader about Mrs Dubose?

The writer uses the simile 'like a glacier', which has connotations of ....

....

This suggests to the reader ....

....

....

Now read this short extract, also from source 10, *To Kill a Mockingbird*, then answer Questions 2 and 3.

> From time to time she would open her mouth wide, and I could see her tongue undulate faintly. Cords of saliva would collect on her lips; she would draw them in, then open her mouth again. Her mouth seemed to have a private existence of its own. It worked separate and apart from the rest of her, out and in, like a clam hole at low tide. Occasionally it would say, 'Pt,' like some viscous substance coming to a boil.

2 Identify at least one simile from the extract above. Write one or two sentences commenting on why the writer has used it and its effect on the reader.

....

....

....

3 Identify the metaphor the writer has used in the extract above. (Hint: look closely at the second sentence.) Write a P-E-E paragraph explaining why the writer has used it and its effect on the reader.

> Don't just identify and name a figurative device used in a text. Remember to comment on the effect the device has on the reader.

....

....

....

....

....

Creation of character

Read this short extract from source 10, *To Kill a Mockingbird*, then answer Question 1.

> 'So you brought that dirty little sister of yours, did you?' was her greeting.
>
> Jem said quietly, 'My sister ain't dirty and I ain't scared of you,' although I noticed that his knees were shaking.
>
> I was expecting a tirade, but all she said was, 'You may commence reading, Jeremy.'

Guided

1 In the source above, the writer uses dialogue to create ideas about the characters. What ideas does this use of dialogue give the reader about Mrs Dubose and Jem?

The writer uses dialogue to show that Mrs Dubose is rude as she calls Jem's sister 'dirty'.

However, Jem's dialogue shows that he is ....

....

....

....

....

Now read this short extract, also from *To Kill a Mockingbird*, then answer Question 2.

> I didn't look any more than I had to. Jem re-opened *Ivanhoe* and began reading. I tried to keep up with him, but he read too fast. When Jem came to a word he didn't know, he skipped it, but Mrs Dubose would catch him and make him spell it out. Jem read for perhaps twenty minutes, during which time I looked at the soot-stained mantelpiece, out of the window, anywhere to keep from looking at her. As he read along, I noticed that Mrs Dubose's corrections grew fewer and farther between, that Jem had even left one sentence dangling in mid-air. She was not listening.

2 How do Jem's actions in the extract above build up an idea of his character?

....

....

....

....

Turn to the full extract from *To Kill a Mockingbird*, in source 10 on page 103. Read lines 22 to 39, focusing on the description of Mrs Dubose. Then answer Question 3.

> Character can be created through dialogue, description or action.

3 Write a P-E-E paragraph about how the writer creates ideas about the character of Mrs Dubose.

....

....

....

....

....

Creating atmosphere

Read this short extract from source 9, *Enduring Love*, then answer Questions 1 to 3.

(20th)

> The wind renewed its (rage) in the treetops just before I felt its (force) on my back. Then it (struck) the balloon which ceased its innocent comical wagging and was suddenly stilled. Its only motion was a shimmer of strain that rippled out across its ridged surface as the contained energy accumulated. It broke free, the anchor flew up in a spray of dirt, and the balloon and basket rose ten feet in the air. The boy was thrown back, out of sight. The pilot had the rope in his hands and was lifted two feet clear off the ground. If Logan had not reached him and taken hold of one of the many dangling lines the balloon would have carried the boy away. Instead, both men were now being pulled across the field, and the farm workers and I were running again.

1 What are the connotations of the words circled in the extract above?

'rage' ....

'force' ....

'struck' ....

2 Look at the first half of the source above, up to the words 'rose ten feet in the air'. Find and circle examples of the following: action verbs, personification, adjectives.

3 In the answer extracts below, students have commented on the atmosphere in the first half of the extract from *Enduring Love*. They have used their answers to Questions 1 and 2 in their writing.

A

> A tense atmosphere is created by the writer using the word 'rage'. This suggests the wind is angry.

B

> The writer creates a tense atmosphere by personifying the wind. It is said to be in a 'rage' and to create a 'force'. This suggests that it is actually fighting the narrator and this is emphasised by use of the action verb 'struck'.

C

> The atmosphere is tense. This is shown by the use of personification of the wind and by the use of strong verbs like 'struck' and 'broke'.
>
> The writer also uses adjectives to show the wind is strong, like 'rippled' and 'ridged'.

(a) Circle the answer extract you think is most effective (A, B or C).

(b) Explain why you feel your chosen answer extract is the most effective.

....

....

....

Read the second half of the extract from *Enduring Love* above, from the words 'The boy was thrown back' to '...were running again'. Then answer Question 4.

> When you answer a question about language techniques in the exam, start with an overview to summarise the overall effect of the source.

⟩ **Guided** ⟩ **4** Using your answers to Questions 1 to 3, write an overview sentence that sums up the overall atmosphere created in the source at the top of this page.

Overall, the writer creates an atmosphere of ....

....

....

Narrative voice

Read extracts 1, 2 and 3 below.

Extract A: from source 9, *Enduring Love*

I should make something clear. There may have been a vague communality of purpose, but we were never a team. There was no chance, no time. Coincidences of time and place, a predisposition to help had brought us together under the balloon. No one was in charge – or everyone was, and we were in a shouting match. The pilot, red-faced, bawling and sweating, we ignored. Incompetence came off him like heat.   But we were beginning to bawl our own instructions too. I know that if I had been uncontested leader the tragedy would not have happened.

Extract B: from source 11, *The Day of the Triffids*

I woke up to find myself in bed, with my mother, my father, and the doctor watching me anxiously My head felt as if it were split open, I was aching all over, and, as I later discovered, one side of my face was decorated with a blotchy-red raised weal. The insistent questions as to how I came to be lying unconscious in the garden were quite useless; I had no faintest idea what it was that had hit me.

Extract C: from source 8, *One Day in the Life of Ivan Denisovich*

Shukhov never overslept reveille. He always got up at once, for the next ninety minutes, until they assembled for work, belonged to him, not to the authorities, and any old-timer could always earn a bit – by sewing a pair of over-mittens for someone out of old sleeve lining …

Now read the descriptions of narrative voice below, then answer Questions 1 and 2.

(a)

First-person narrative has been used to allow the reader to know the narrator's feelings about the other characters.

(b)

Third-person narrative has been used. This 'omniscient narrator' knows everything, including the narrator's feelings and motives.

(c)

First-person narrative has been used to keep some of the details from the reader. This increases the tension.

1 Match each extract (A, B, C) above to one of the descriptions of narrative voice outlined in (a), (b) and (c). Write the letters of the descriptions in the spaces below to make the matches.

Extract A: ....

Extract B: ....

Extract C: ....

> Narrative voice is the 'voice' a writer of fiction chooses to tell the story. A writer can choose a narrative voice to create a particular point of view.

2 Reread Extract A. How has the first person narrative voice been used to suggest that the main character views himself as the most effective of the rescuers?

....

....

....

Putting it into practice

Read the full extract from *Enduring Love*, source 9 on page 102, then answer the exam-style question below.

2. Look in detail at this extract from **lines 1 to 13** of the source.

How does the writer use language here to create a sense of drama and tension?

You could include the writer's choice of:

- words and phrases
- language features and techniques
- sentence forms.

(8 marks)

When you tackle this type of question in the exam, remember to:

- spend around 8 minutes on your answer
- read the question carefully and highlight the main focus
- read the source text thoroughly, annotating as you read
- only use the lines of the text referred to in the question
- identify the language and structural devices used and comment on their effects
- support all your points with clear evidence and a clear explanation by using a P-E-E structure in your paragraphs.

In the exam you will need to write about structure to answer this kind of question. Structure is covered later in this Workbook. Here, you just need to comment on how the writer uses language — skills you have covered on pages 19 to 24.

....

....

....

....

....

....

....

....

....

....

....

....

....

....

Remember: You have more space than this to answer your question in the exam. Use your own paper to finish your answer to the question above.

Had a go ☐   Nearly there ☐   Nailed it! ☐

Putting it into practice

Read the full extract from 'Occupations Accessible to Women: Elementary Teaching' in source 12a on page 105, then answer the exam-style question below.

Paper

3. You now need to refer **only** to **source 12a**.

How does the narrator use language to reveal the benefits of teaching?   **(12 marks)**

When you tackle this type of question in the exam, remember to:

- spend around 12 minutes on your answer
- read the question carefully and highlight the main focus
- read the source text thoroughly, annotating as you read
- only use the lines of the text referred to in the question
- identify the language and structural devices used and comment on their effects
- support all your points with clear evidence and a clear explanation by using a P-E-E structure in your paragraphs.

....

....

....

....

....

....

....

....

....

....

....

....

....

....

....

....

....

....

Remember: You have more space than this to answer your question in the exam. Use your own paper to finish your answer to the question above.

Rhetorical devices 1

Read this short extract from source 12b, 'OK, you try teaching 13-year-olds', then answer Questions 1 and 2.

21st

Shocking news: a young trainee languages teacher on placement at Tarleton High in Lancashire "lost it" in class, barricaded the door with furniture, trapping the pupils, and threatened to kill them with something nasty that she had in her handbag. But why shocking? Imagine yourself in her place, "teaching" about 30 13- or 14-year-old creatures. Do you have one or two in your house? Are they polite, quiet and cooperative? Or are they breathtakingly insolent, noisy, crabby, offensive, skulking, smoking, drugging, and whingeing that they are not suitably entertained? What if you had 30? Wouldn't you like something in your handbag to shut the little toads up?

1 Find one example each in the source above for four of the five rhetorical devices listed below.

• pattern of three ....

• lists ....

• alliteration ....

• rhetorical questions ....

• colloquial language ....

Guided 2 For each device you have identified, write one or two sentences commenting on:
• why the writer has used it
• the intended effect on the reader.

The answer has been started for you, with comments about the writer's use of lists.

> Remember to think about how rhetorical devices are used by considering their effect on the reader.

The writer uses a list of negative adjectives, such as 'insolent, noisy' and 'crabby' to emphasise

how difficult teenagers can be. As this list comes after the description of the teacher's actions,

it might make readers feel some sympathy for teachers. The writer also uses ....

....

....

....

....

....

....

....

....

....

....

....

Rhetorical devices 2

Read this short extract from source 13a, *The Boys Are Back in Town* by Simon Carr, then answer Question 1.

> Mothers tend to a different theory. They take a more active interest in the details and the way stations through the day. Mothers like a routine; they even say that children like a routine ('It gives them security'). The bath before bedtime calms them down. This may be true, too, but in our house there aren't bedtimes, let alone baths before them.

1 The writer has a very relaxed attitude to parenting. How does the repetition of 'Mothers' and 'routine' help to show this attitude?

....

....

....

Now read the first three sentences of the next paragraph from *The Boys Are Back in Town*, up to the words 'they drive you nuts'. Then answer Question 2.

> The canon law my boys operate to is <u>listed here in no particular order.</u> No interrupting adults. Of course we like talking to children and we like them talking to us, but those demands for food, drink or attention that come in from nowhere, unasked, unexpected, they drive you nuts. Yes, and no swearing if you're a child not even words that sound like swearing. Except damn, of course, and hell. What else? As little stealing and lying as possible. No wanton littering, no fighting except for fun or out of earshot. Be polite as much as possible – of course, you can't when you're very angry. You must work hard at school. Screaming insanely, running round the house making absurd and disgusting noises, sliding in the mud in the park after dark and throwing water bombs and tennis balls at windows – all these were encouraged.

2 The underlined section in the extract above provides a contrast (an opposing or different idea) to the ideas mothers have about parenting in the first extract on this page. Write one or two sentences explaining how this use of contrast helps to demonstrate the writer's relaxed attitude to his children.

....

....

....

Read the rest of the extract from *The Boys Are Back in Town* above, from the words 'Yes, and no swearing' to 'all these were encouraged'. Then answer Question 3.

> If you know it, use the technical name for the device in your answer. If you don't know the technical name, you should still comment on the language and its effect.

3 Identify one example of hyperbole and one example of emotive language in the second extract above. Write one or two sentences commenting on why the writer has used each rhetorical device and the effect each one has on the reader.

Hyperbole: ....

....

Emotive language: ....

....

Whole text structure: fiction

Read the full extract from *Enduring Love*, in source 9 on page 102. Now focus on these lines from the source, before answering Questions 1 and 2.

20th

> What we saw when we stood from our picnic was this: a huge grey balloon, the size of a house, the shape of a tear drop, had come down in the field. <u>The pilot must have been half way out of the passenger basket as it touched the ground. His leg had become entangled in a rope that was attached to an anchor.</u> Now, as the wind gusted, and pushed and lifted the balloon towards the escarpment, he was being half dragged, half carried across the field. In the basket was a child, a boy of about ten.

1 How do the sentences underlined above foreshadow the drama that follows later in the source?

....

....

Guided

2 In the source above, why does the writer leave the information about the boy in the basket until after he has written about the wind?

The writer withholds the fact that there is a boy in the basket as this structure increases the

tension for the reader. Before this fact is revealed, the writer closely describes ....

....

....

The revelation that there is a boy in the basket increases the tension because ....

....

....

Now focus on what happens next in the source, before answering Question 3.

20th

> In a sudden lull, the man was on his feet, clutching at the basket, or at the boy. Then there was another gust, and the pilot was on his back, bumping over the rough ground, trying to dig his feet in for purchase, or lunging for the anchor behind him in order to secure it in the earth. Even if he had been able, he would not have dared disentangle himself from the anchor rope. He needed his weight to keep the balloon on the ground, and the wind could have snatched the rope from his hands.

3 Here, the writer describes the actions of the man and what happens to the balloon in great detail. What is the effect of this structure on the reader?

....

....

....

....

....

> Remember that writers of fiction use a variety of narrative structures for effect. These include foreshadowing, use of closely described detail or action, repetition and dialogue.

Whole text structure: non-fiction

Read this short extract from source 12b, 'OK, you try teaching 13-year-olds' by Michele Hanson, then answer Question 1.

> **21st**
>
> Shocking news: a young trainee languages teacher on placement at Tarleton High in Lancashire "lost it" in class, barricaded the door with furniture, trapping the pupils, and threatened to kill them with something nasty that she had in her handbag.

1 The opening of any text needs to engage the reader. In the extract above, the writer chooses to use the opening to set the scene. How has she ensured that readers will want to read on?

....

....

Now read the full extract from 'OK, you try teaching 13-year-olds' on page 106. Then answer Question 2.

2 Consider the following ways in which writers can end their writing in order to leave a lasting impression:

| vivid images | warnings | calls to action | positivity | summary of main points made |

Circle the one you think most suits the way Michele Hanson ends her article and explain why you think she chose to end it that way.

....

....

Read this short extract from source 14a, ''Appy ever after' by John Arlidge:

> **21st**
>
> The trouble is, Goldwasser has just attached two electrodes to my head and is about to start pumping electricity straight into my brain.

Now read this second short extract, from later in the same article, before answering Question 3. The electricity is now flowing through the electrodes into Arlidge's head:

> **21st**
>
> And then something remarkable happens. After a few minutes I begin to feel waves gently flowing through my head. I don't notice at first but soon I begin to slump in my chair, my pupils dilate and my breathing slows.

Guided ▷ **3** Writers need to keep the interest of their readers and they often do it by changing the tone in the middle section of their writing. How does Arlidge do this in the extracts from his article above?

Initially, Arlidge is scared about the idea of having two electrodes attached to his head. This is

implied in the phrase 'pumping electricity straight into my brain'. However, when he actually tries

the electrodes, his tone changes ....

....

....

....

Identifying sentence types

Look at the sentences below, then answer the questions that follow.

A   My hands were trembling.

B   Even though I had done this hundreds of times before, I was still terrified.

C   My blood ran cold and my heart stopped.

D   Blind terror.

1 Look carefully at the four sentences above. Each one is a different type of sentence. But which is which?

   Sentence .... is a single-clause sentence.

   Sentence .... is a multi-clause sentence (coordinate).

   Sentence .... is a multi-clause sentence (subordinate).

   Sentence .... is a minor sentence.

Now read this short extract from 'OK, you try teaching 13-year-olds', then answer Question **2**.

Now think of that young teacher. "She had been trying to get them to be quiet," we learn. So she had probably been shouted at and humiliated for 40 minutes. This was her very last day of several horrible weeks of a placement. The end of her torment was a whisker away, but, driven barmy by pupils, she still blew it. Her career is now ruined. But the children were "petrified … burst into tears" and were offered "support". The pathetic little wets. She was pretending, you fools – dredging up a last desperate ploy to shut the monsters up. If she had cried, they would have laughed out loud. Hopefully, she won't be sacked. If that's what she really, really wants.

2 In the extract above, highlight or circle one example of each kind of sentence: single-clause, multi-clause (subordinate), multi-clause (coordinate) and minor.

SINGLE-CLAUSE sentences are made up of just **one clause** and provide **one piece of information** about an event or action. They contain **a subject** and **one verb**.
MULTI-CLAUSE sentences are made up of **more than one clause**. They contain **two or more verbs**.
SUBORDINATE clauses do not make sense on their own. They are **dependent** on the main clause.
COORDINATE clauses are an **equal pair**, where neither clause is dependent on the other.
MINOR SENTENCES are grammatically incomplete because they **do not contain a verb**.

Commenting on sentences

Read this short extract from source 14a, ''Appy ever after', then answer Question 1.

21st

> He hands me the controller. I select Calm mode. I turn the dial up and – *Holy silicon mad professors!* – it hurts. There's a sharp vibration that feels like the neurons in my head are pogoing. Not relaxing at all. I turn it down and wait. And then something remarkable happens. After a few minutes, I begin to feel waves gently flowing through my head. I don't notice at first but soon I begin to slump in my chair, my pupils dilate and my breathing slows.

1 The source above starts with short sentences and ends with a long sentence that has several subordinate clauses. How do these sentence structures suggest what is happening to the narrator's feelings?

....

....

....

....

....

Now read this short extract from source 9, *Enduring Love*, then answer Question 2.

20th

> I got there before them. When I took a rope the basket was above head height. The boy inside it was screaming. Despite the wind, I caught the smell of urine. Jed Parry was on a rope seconds after me and the two farm workers, Joseph Lacey and Toby Greene, caught hold just after him. Greene was having a coughing fit, but he kept his grip. The pilot was shouting instructions at us, but too frantically, and no one was listening.

Guided **2** In this source, the writer uses a variety of sentence lengths to create a sense of tension. Explain how the sentence structures create tension.

The writer starts the paragraph with a short, single-clause sentence ....

....

....

....

After using short sentences, the writer then uses a multi-clause sentence. This adds to the

tension ....

....

....

....

The writer then uses two multi-clause sentences that end with subordinate clauses. This adds

to the tension ....

....

....

....

Putting it into practice

Read the full extract from source 11, *The Day of the Triffids* on page 104, then answer the exam-style question below.

Paper 1

3. You now need to think about the **whole** of the **source**.

How has the writer structured the text to interest you as a reader?

You could write about:

- what the writer focuses your attention on at the beginning
- how and why the writer changes this focus as the extract develops
- any other structural features that interest you.

(8 marks)

When you tackle this type of question in the exam, remember to:

- spend around 8 minutes on your answer
- read the question carefully and highlight the main focus
- read the source text thoroughly, annotating as you read
- refer to the whole of the source
- identify the structural devices used and comment on their effects.

....
....
....
....
....
....
....
....
....
....
....
....
....
....
....
....
....
....

Remember: You have more space than this to answer your question in the exam. Use your own paper to finish your answer to the question above.

Putting it into practice

Read the full extract from ''Appy ever after', in source 14a on page 109, then answer the exam-style question below.

**Paper
②**

3. You now need to refer **only** to **source 14a**.

How does John Arlidge use language to engage his reader in the mood-altering techniques?

(12 marks)

> When you tackle this type of question in the exam, remember to:
>
> · spend around 12 minutes on your answer
>
> · read the question carefully and highlight the main focus
>
> · read the source text thoroughly, annotating as you read
>
> · identify the language and structural devices used and comment on their effects.

....

....

....

....

....

....

....

....

....

....

....

....

....

....

....

....

....

....

....

....

> **Remember:** You have more space than this to answer your question in the exam. Use your own paper to finish your answer to the question above.

Evaluating a fiction text 1

Read the full extract from *Enduring Love*, in source 9 on page 102. Then read the exam-style question below. **You don't need to answer this question**. Instead, think about what it is asking you to do, then answer Question 1.

Paper
①

> **4.** Focus this part of your answer on the final twenty lines of the source, **from line 29 to the end**.
> A student, having read this section of the text said: "In these lines, the narrator is shown to be a natural leader."
> To what extent do you agree with this view?
> In your response, you could:
> • write about your own impressions of the narrator
> • evaluate how the writer has created these impressions
> • support your opinions with quotations from the text.   **(20 marks)**

1 Which of the following should you do when answering an evaluation question? Circle your choices.

| Focus closely on the specific lines given in the question, but also look at the whole text. | Use evidence from the text. | Focus closely on individual words and phrases, explaining connotations in detail. | Consider both sides of the argument when expressing your opinion. | Read the question carefully to make sure you evaluate the right aspect of the text. |

Below you will see an extract from a student's answer to Question 4 above. In the answer, the student is referring to this short section of source 9, *Enduring Love*:

> (20th)
> <u>We were all talking at once</u>. Two of us, <u>myself and the motorist</u>, wanted to walk the balloon away from the edge. <u>Someone</u> thought the priority was to get the boy out. <u>Someone</u> else was calling for the balloon to be pulled down so that we could anchor it firmly. I saw no contradiction, for we could be pulling the balloon down as we moved back into the field.

The narrator does not appear to be a natural leader at the start of this section as he ....

....

However, <u>he then puts himself first when explaining an idea</u>, for example ....

....

<u>The writer uses repetition</u> to ....

....

Guided   **2** (a) Match the underlined sections of the student's answer to the underlined phrases in the short extract.

  (b) Complete the student answer, adding evidence from the short extract above from source 9, *Enduring Love*, and explanations to evaluate the source.

When you evaluate, you need to comment on whether the impressions you get from the lines given in the question are similar to or different from the impressions you get from the whole of the source. Reread the full extract from *Enduring Love*, source 9 on page 102.

3 Does the whole extract suggest the narrator is a natural leader? Select one piece of evidence to back up your impression.

....

....

> Use quotations to back up your points but you don't need to analyse the language or structure in detail.

Evaluating a fiction text 2

To evaluate a fiction text effectively, you need to carefully consider a range of alternative interpretations, and justify your opinions by using evidence from the text to support or challenge the statement provided in the question.

Read the full extract from *To Kill a Mockingbird*, in source 10 on page 103, then read the exam-style question below and complete the table, using evidence carefully to support or challenge the statement made. A couple of examples have been completed for you.

Paper ① ▷Guided▷

4. Focus this part of your answer on the second half of the source, **from line 22 to the end**.

A student, having read this section of the text, said: "The writer has presented Mrs Dubose in a sympathetic light so that the reader feels sympathy for her situation."

To what extent do you agree?

In your response, you could:

- write about your own impressions of Mrs Dubose
- evaluate how the writer has created these impressions
- support your opinions with quotations from the text. **(20 marks)**

Planning template:

Mrs Dubose is presented sympathetically			
Yes		**No**	
"Come closer," said Mrs Dubose. "Come to the side of the bed."	This affectionate phrase suggests that Mrs Dubose is in need of company and is lonely, therefore increasing our sympathy for her.	"Mrs Dubose would catch him and make him spell it out"	This suggests that Mrs Dubose is threatening and demanding, which reduces our sympathy for her.

Remember to use comparative adverbials for the evaluation question as it will encourage you to produce a debate that considers alternative interpretations of the text.

Using evidence to evaluate

When using evidence for the evaluation question, it is important to consider the different ways you can use quotations to support or reject the statement provided in the question. The same quotation can sometimes be used to support or reject the viewpoint put forward in the question as long as you clearly explain how it relates to your evaluation.

Study the student annotations below. Students have been asked whether they agree or not that Shukhov in *One day in the Life of Ivan Denisovich* is presented as someone the reader can admire. The annotations around the chosen quotation have been used both to agree and disagree with the question.

20th

> No wonder the team-leader looked so worried, that was his responsibility – to elbow some other team, some bunch of clod-hoppers, into the assignment instead of the 104th. Of course he wouldn't get the authorities to agree if he turned up empty-handed. He'd have to take a pound of pork-fat to the senior official there, if not a couple of pounds.
>
> There's never any harm in trying, so why not have a go at the sick-bay and get a few days off if you can? After all, he did feel as though every limb was out of joint.

Yes, you could use this quotation to support the idea that Shukhov is using his initiative to make life less arduous for himself by using a bribe of pork-fat. The vivid description of his limbs being out of joint means that we are encouraged to understand his actions of trying to survive in that environment.

The narrator is clearly a deceptive and untrustworthy character and is disloyal to his fellow workers, based on the way he bribes his supervisor and is planning to lie about his illness. It seems as if he is trying to justify his actions by complaining 'every limb was out of joint'.

1 Reread the second half of source 11, *The Day of the Triffids* on page 104, from line 42 to the end. Provide evidence to support and challenge the following statement: "The narrator is presented as foolish, rather than adventurous." Find a quotation and annotate it in the same way as the example.

....

....

....

....

....

....

....

You can use longer quotations, but if you do you must be very careful about layout.

2 Which of the following should you not do when using a longer quotation? Circle your choice(s).

(a) Introduce it with a colon.

(b) Include it as part of your sentence.

(c) Start the quotation on a new line.

(d) Put the quotation in quotation marks.

> When using quotations, remember that:
> - short quotations are most effective
> - you must use quotations rather than paraphrasing when explaining the effects of language
> - all quotations must be in quotation marks and copied correctly from the text.

Putting it into practice

Read the full extract from *One Day in the Life of Ivan Denisovich*, source 8 on page 101, then answer the exam-style question below.

Paper 1

4. Focus this part of your answer on the second half of the source, **from line 26 to the end**.

A student, having read this section of the text said: "The writer encourages the reader to feel that Shukhov has found a way to deal with the hardship of the camp."

To what extent do you agree?

In your response, you could:

- write about your own impressions of Shukhov
- evaluate how the writer has created these impressions
- support your opinions with quotations from the text. **(20 marks)**

When you tackle this type of question in the exam, remember to:

- spend around 20 minutes on your answer
- read the question carefully and highlight the main focus
- read the source text thoroughly, annotating as you read
- only use the lines of the text referred to in the question
- use inference and evidence from the text to explain your ideas and assess the effect of the text.

....

....

....

....

....

....

....

....

....

....

....

....

....

....

....

....

Remember: You have more space than this to answer your question in the exam. Use your own paper to finish your answer to the question above.

Writing about two texts

In Paper 2, two assessment objectives will test your ability to handle two texts together. These are Assessment objectives 1 (b) and 3. Read the assessment objectives, then answer Questions 1 and 2.

Assessment objective 1 (b)

Select and synthesise evidence from different texts

Assessment objective 3

Compare writers' ideas and perspectives, as well as how these are conveyed, across two or more texts

1 Circle the word below which is **not** a synonym for 'synthesise'.

combine	fuse	amalgamate	blend	mix	separate

> The texts in Paper 2 may be similar or different in various ways. Think about:
> * the ideas they express about the topic
> * their points of view
> * the language they use
> * how they are structured.

2 Which of the assessment objectives above will require you to identify **and** explain both similarities **and** differences between the two texts? ....

Now look at these exam-style questions. **You don't need to answer these questions.** Instead, think about how they test the skills in Assessment objectives 1 (b) and 3 and then answer Question 3.

Paper
(2)

2. Use details from **both** sources. Write a summary of the different rules for bringing up children.   **(8 marks)**

4. Compare how the two writers convey their different attitudes to parenting and education.
   In your answer, you could:
   * compare their different attitudes
   * compare the methods they use to convey their attitudes
   * support your ideas with quotations from both texts.   **(16 marks)**

3 Read the statements below. Decide which paper or question each statement describes.
   Circle your choices.
   (a) The two non-fiction texts will always be linked by a common theme or topic, so they will
       always have something in common.   **Paper 1   Paper 2**
   (b) This question will test Assessment objective 3 by asking you to compare the texts.
                                                                        Question 2   Question 4
   (c) This question will test Assessment objective 1 (b) by asking you to synthesise information
       from both texts.   **Question 2   Question 4**
   (d) This question is worth only 8 marks, so you should only make about two or three points.
                                                                        Question 2   Question 4
   (e) This question is worth 16 marks, so you should spend more time on this question.
                                                                        Question 2   Question 4
   (f) For this question, you will need to compare the language used as well as looking at the
       writers' attitudes and ideas.   **Question 2   Question 4**

Selecting evidence for synthesis

When selecting information for the synthesis question (question 2 in Paper 2), you need to choose evidence that is relevant to the question. Read the exam-style question below. **You don't need to answer this question**. Instead, think about what it is asking you to do, then answer Questions 1 and 2.

Paper ②

> **2.** You need to refer to **source 14a** and **source 14b** for this question.
> Use details from **both** sources. Write a summary of the positive aspects of mind-altering techniques.   **(8 marks)**

1 Underline or highlight the key words in exam-style Question 2.

2 Look at the short extracts below. Which ones would be a good source of relevant quotations in answer to Question 2 above? Circle one extract from each text.

(a) Extracts from source 14a, ''Appy ever after'

> **i** Goldwasser believes harnessing willpower will have big implications in the treatment of obesity, alcoholism or gambling addiction…

> **ii** Thync is focusing on willpower, self-control, motivation, confidence and creativity.

(b) Extracts from source 14b, 'Victorian Hypnotism'

> **i** Legs and breasts may be amputated, children born, teeth extracted, in short the most painful experiences undergone, with no other anæsthetic than the hypnotizer's assurance that no pain shall be felt. Similarly morbid pains may be annihilated, neuralgias, toothaches, rheumatisms cured.

> **ii** Hallucinations and histrionic delusions generally go with a certain depth of the trance, and are followed by complete forgetfulness.

> As only 8 marks are available for the synthesis question, skim read the texts to save time.

Now read the full extracts in source 13a, *The Boys Are Back in Town* on page 107, and source 13b, 'The Rearing and Management of Children' on page 108. Then read the exam-style question below. **You don't need to answer this question**. Instead, think about what it is asking you to do, then answer Question 3.

Paper ②

> **2.** You need to refer to **source 13a** and **source 13b** for this question.
> Use details from **both** sources. Write a summary of the rules for mothers bringing up children.   **(8 marks)**

3 Both texts suggest that mothers follow strict rules and routines for bringing up children. Write out the evidence that supports this similarity.

....

....

....

Answering a synthesis question

When you are synthesising the evidence you have selected from the two non-fiction texts in Paper 2, you need to use suitable adverbials and linking phrases.

> **Guided**

1 Tick or circle the adverbials and linking phrases below that are suitable for synthesising evidence. Two examples have been done for you.

| similarly | on the other hand | (likewise) | both | in the same way | however | (also) |

2 Why should you use adverbials in your synthesis of evidence?

....

....

To show your full understanding of the synthesis question, you should start your answer with an overview. Read the exam-style question below. **You don't need to answer this question now.** Instead, think about what it is asking you to do, then answer Question 3.

Paper ②

2. Use details from **both** sources. Write a summary of the positive aspects of mind-altering techniques.   **(8 marks)**

3 Look at the overviews below, written by students in response to exam-style Question 2 above.

A Both writers write about mind-altering techniques.

B Both writers write about mind-altering techniques, one writes about hypnosis and the other about a mind-altering machine.

C Both writers feel that mind-altering techniques can have a positive impact on health and happiness.

(a) Tick or circle the overview that you think is most effective.

(b) Explain why the overview you have chosen would be the best way to start an answer to Question 2 above.

....

....

4 Read the full extracts in source 14a, ''Appy ever after' by John Arlidge on page 109 and source 14b, 'Victorian Hypnotism' on page 110. Then write one synthesis paragraph in answer to exam-style Question 2 above.

- Use suitable adverbials and linking phrases from the selection at the top of this page.
- Start your paragraph with the overview you chose for Question 3.
- You could use the evidence you identified on page 40.

> Try to make each sentence cover both texts. Use short quotations where possible, or paraphrase the text if a quotation would be too long.

....

....

....

....

Looking closely at language

Read this short extract from source 14a, "Appy ever after', then answer Questions 1 to 3.

> **21st**
>
> Goldwasser and Tyler may sound (bonkers), but if their timing is anything to go by, they're the smartest guys in the lab. Wearable (gizmos) are the hottest new sector in the trillion-pound global technology sector. Apple launches its first smartwatch in the new year and will be followed by (wearable kit) from Microsoft and Google, which promises new versions of its web-enabled spectacles, Google Glass. Many of the new devices are designed to improve our health by monitoring our blood pressure and our stress levels, keeping tabs on how much exercise we take and helping us to feel refreshed in the morning by waking us up as we are coming out of a period of deep sleep.

Guided

1 What are the connotations of the words and phrases circled in the extract above? The first one has been done for you.

'bonkers' This means 'mad', 'crazy' or 'wild'. It's an informal term so it could have positive connotations.

'gizmos' ....

'wearable kit' ....

2 Write one or two sentences explaining the effect created by the words and phrases circled in the source. Use the words and phrases as quotations and make sure you refer to their connotations.

....

....

....

3 The final sentence (underlined in the source above) is very long and has several subordinate clauses. How does this sentence change the tone of this short extract?

....

....

....

Now read this short extract, also from "Appy ever after', then answer Question 4.

> **21st**
>
> Goldwasser and Tyler are taking the idea one step further, giving us the power to change the way we feel, whenever we want.
>
> "Tap into your self-control. Tap into your creativity. Tap into your energy. Tap into your calm. Think of us as your third cup of coffee in the morning or your glass of wine at night," Goldwasser smiles.

4 Look at the language and sentence structure in the above source.

(a) Identify the rhetorical device used. Write a sentence commenting on the effect it creates.

....

....

(b) Explain the effect created by the sentence structure.

....

....

> When answering a comparison question in the exam, you should always look for similarities and differences between the language of the two texts. You must not write about one text without making a comparison point about the other. Try to give the texts equal weighting in your answer.

Planning to compare language

Read the short extracts 1 and 2 below. Then answer Question 1.

Extract 1: from source 12a, 'Occupations Accessible to Women'

The duties of teachers in elementary schools are both healthful and congenial. The hours of work vary in some schools according to the season of the year, but usually the children assemble at 9:30 a.m. and are dismissed at 4:30 p.m. A quarter of an hour's run is allowed them at eleven, and an hour and a quarter (sometimes more) for dinner, thus reducing the actual school hours to five hours and a half. After school the hours are free for recreation, pleasant visits, or study.

Extract 2: from source 12b, 'OK, you try teaching 13-year-olds'

I'm trying not to sound bitter here, but I have taught; I have known supply-teaching hell; and I, too, have blown my top, even though it was 3.30pm and nearly over, because by then they were still climbing up walls (really), throwing scissors, dribbling glue and screaming all the while … and when that happens, sometimes one just cannot keep one's cool a second longer.

And 13 is a particularly cruel age. In my first year's teaching, I crashed the car and sliced my forehead open on the sun-visor. Back at school, with my unsightly 27-stitch scar, I passed two 13-year-old girls. "She looks uglier than ever," said they, laughing merrily.

> **Guided**

1 Now look at one student's plan for comparing the language in the two texts, and its effects. The plan is incomplete. Add as many details as you can, for example, quotations and explanations.

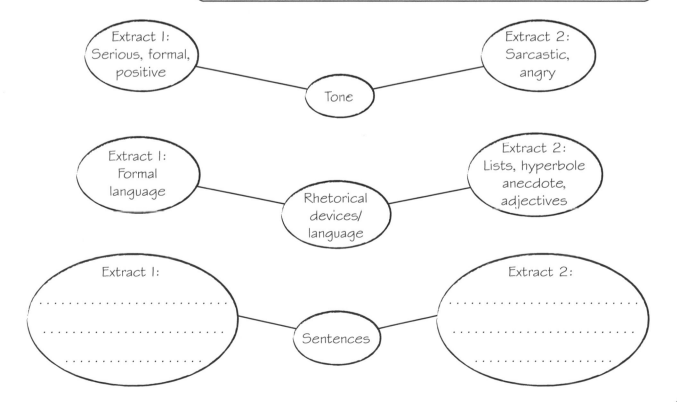

When comparing you can:
* start with the language and structural techniques the texts have in common, then compare the effects created
OR
* start with similarities in the effects of the two texts (for example, tone), then compare the techniques the writers have used to create those effects.

Extract 1: Serious, formal, positive — **Tone** — Extract 2: Sarcastic, angry

Extract 1: Formal language — **Rhetorical devices/ language** — Extract 2: Lists, hyperbole anecdote, adjectives

Extract 1: .... — **Sentences** — Extract 2: ....

43

Comparing language

Read Extracts 1 and 2 below. Then answer the questions that follow.

Extract 1: from source 13b, 'The Rearing and Management of Children'

It is commonly believed that no harm can come of letting a child have its own way, so long as it is a mere babe. But this is a serious delusion. As soon as a child is of an age to express its wants, whether by one means or another, it is old enough to be brought into habits of obedience. Obedience is the first lesson to be taught and very sensible are all well-managed babes of its meaning. No harsh words, no impatient gestures, need be added to enforce the rule, which consists simply in not doing as the babe demands, if it be not the right time and the proper place for the desired gratification.

Extract 2: from source 13a, *The Boys are Back in Town*

Mothers tend to a different theory. They take a more active interest in the details and the way stations through the day. Mothers like a routine; they even say that children like a routine ('It gives them security'). This may be true, too, but in our house there aren't bedtimes, let alone baths before them.

The canon law my boys operate to is listed here in no particular order. No interrupting adults. Of course we like talking to children and we like them talking to us, but those demands for food, drink or attention that come in from nowhere, unasked, unexpected, they drive you nuts. Yes, and no swearing if you're a child not even words that sound like swearing. Except damn, of course, and hell. What else? As little stealing and lying as possible. No wanton littering, no fighting except for fun or out of earshot. Be polite as much as possible – of course, you can't when you're very angry. You must work hard at school. Screaming insanely, running round the house making absurd and disgusting noises, sliding in mud in the park after dark and throwing water bombs and tennis balls at windows – all these were encouraged.

> **Guided**

1 List two similar language features in the two extracts and explain the effect they have.

  (a) Language feature short sentences   Effect ....

  ....

  (b) Language feature ....   Effect ....

  ....

2 (a) Identify the purpose or effect of the two texts.

  ....

  (b) What is the language technique used in Extract 1 to achieve this effect?

  Extract 1: ....

  ....

  (c) What is the language technique used in Extract 2 to achieve this effect?

  Extract 2: ....

  ....

Comparing structure

> **Guided**

It is important that you are able to compare how the texts are structured and how this has an impact on the reader. An example of how you can compare the way the two texts are structured is shown below. Read through the examples then complete the analysis of the way the texts conclude.

	Source 12a	Comparing structure	Source 12b
Title	'Occupations Accessible to Women'		'OK, you try teaching 13-year-olds'
Beginning	THE great difficulty of the educational question in the present day, and the obstacle to complete success in the earnest efforts made, is the difficulty, almost impossibility, of finding sufficiently-qualified teachers.	Both texts focus on the struggles that are associated with teaching though Cassell's formal introduction is focused on recruitment, whereas Hanson's introduction is more dramatic and personal, encouraging the reader to examine the problem on a more emotional level than Cassell's opening.	Shocking news: a young trainee languages teacher on placement at Tarleton High in Lancashire "lost it" in class, barricaded the door with furniture, trapping the pupils, and threatened to kill them with something nasty that she had in her handbag.
Middle section	The school selected should be taught by a very good certificated master or mistress, where an assistant should be likely to learn the system of school drill and discipline, and also how practically to manage children en masse, according to the latest approved Government rules.	Both writers consider the qualities needed to be a good teacher. Whereas Cassell focuses on the discipline and adhering to rules and regulations, Hanson is more irreverent and informal, using capitals and hyperbole 'you are done for' to create a comic effect on the reader, while still communicating the difficulties teachers face.	To be a teacher, one must be calm, sensible, tough, smartly dressed ALL THE TIME, and attractive. Otherwise, you are done for.
End	The comfort and advantage of possessing a small home would render the position of an elementary school-mistress an eminently tempting one to many a poor governess, could she but manage to qualify herself to hold the position.	....	The end of her torment was a whisker away, but, driven barmy by pupils, she still blew it. Her career is now ruined. But the children were "petrified ... burst into tears" and were offered "support". The pathetic little wets. She was pretending, you fools – dredging up a last desperate ploy to shut the monsters up. If she had cried, they would have laughed out loud. Hopefully, she won't be sacked. If that's what she really, really wants.

Comparing ideas

Read the openings of source 12b, 'OK, you try teaching 13-year-olds' and source 12a 'Occupations Accessible to Women'.

Extract 1: from source 12b, 'OK, you try teaching 13-year-olds' by Michele Hanson

Shocking news: a young trainee languages teacher on placement at Tarleton High in Lancashire "lost it" in class, barricaded the door with furniture, trapping the pupils, and threatened to kill them with something nasty that she had in her handbag. But why shocking? Imagine yourself in her place, "teaching" about 30 13- or 14-year-old creatures.

Extract 2: from source 12a, 'Occupations Accessible to Women' from *Cassell's Household Guide*

THE great difficulty of the educational question in the present day, and the obstacle to complete success in the earnest efforts made, is the difficulty, almost impossibility, of finding sufficiently-qualified teachers. The demand created by the Education Acts is estimated at over 25,000 of both sexes - the women, however, being in the majority.

Guided

1 (a) P-E-E paragraphs are a good way to structure your answer to a comparison question. Finish this point about the ideas expressed in the extracts above:

Both texts start by expressing ideas about ....

....

(b) Now finish the P-E-E paragraph by making a comparison. Add evidence from each extract, and explain how the evidence supports your point above.

Hanson feels ....

....

whereas 'Occupations Accessible to Women' ....

....

Read the full extract in source 12b, 'OK, you try teaching 13-year-olds' on page 106.

2 Identify one more of each writer's ideas. For each one, find a short quotation as evidence.

Text 1:..

....

Text 2:..

....

3 Using your answer to Question 2, choose one idea from each extract. Write a P-E-E paragraph comparing the two texts.

....

....

....

....

Comparing perspective

Read sources 1 and 2 below. They are the opening paragraphs of two texts about parenting. Then answer Questions 1 and 2.

Extract 1: from source 13b, 'The Rearing and Management of Children' from *Cassell's Household Guide*

> **19th**
>
> It is commonly believed that no harm can come of letting a child have its own way, so long as it is a mere babe. But this is a serious delusion.

Extract 2: from source 13a, *The Boys Are Back in Town* by Simon Carr

> **21st**
>
> The fact is, I run a pretty loose ship. There's a lot of give in the structure. In our world of fuzzy logic and more-or-less, we need a lot of give to get by.

1 The opening sentences of Extract 1 from source 13b makes it clear that the writer feels children need rules. How does Simon Carr's perspective on parenting compare with this view?

....

....

....

Guided

2 Complete this comparison explaining how each writer uses language to show their perspective.

In 'The Rearing and Management of Children', the writer uses the emotive phrase 'a serious delusion', which helps to show the writer's strong feelings about obedience. In *The Boys Are Back in Town* ....

....

....

....

Read the full extracts in source 13b, 'The Rearing and Management of Children' on page 108, and source 13a, *The Boys Are Back in Town* on page 107. Pay particular attention to the way they end. Then answer Question 3.

> It is a good idea to look at differences between the beginning and ending of a text when you are thinking about perspective. This will also help you to compare the structure of texts.

3 Write two P-E-E paragraphs comparing the writers' perspectives throughout the sources. Consider whether their perspectives have remained the same throughout or whether they end with a different point of view. Use one piece of evidence from each of the sources.

....

....

....

....

....

Answering a comparison question

When you compare the language used in two texts you can write about:

The main idea: what the texts are about

> Both texts are about ...

> On the other hand, **source Y** explores ...

> **Source X** is about ...

The perspective: the writers' point of view

> The writer of **source X** feels ...

> **Source Y** aims to ...

> negative

> The perspective of the writer is ...

> positive

> The perspective is shown through the writer's use of ...

The effect on the reader:

> create humour

> Both texts aim to engage the reader but do so in different ways.

> influence

> **Source X** engages the reader by ...

> **Source Y**, however, uses ...

> shock

Similar language features:

> lists

> pattern of three

> Both texts use rhetorical questions, but use them to achieve different effects.

> figurative language

> contrast

> **Source X** poses the question ...

> repetition

> emotive language

> **Source Y** uses a rhetorical question to ...

> hyperbole   sentence   structure

> Remember to make direct comparisons and that you can compare similarities and differences between the two texts.

Look again at source 12b, 'OK, you try teaching 13-year-olds' on page 106, and source 12a, 'Occupations Accessible to Women' on page 105. Use the prompts above to write a paragraph comparing the different ways language and structure are used for effect in the two extracts. Remember to use quotations as evidence to support your points.

....

....

....

....

....

....

Putting it into practice

Read source 13a, *The Boys are Back in Town* on page 107, and source 13b, 'The Rearing and Management of Children' on page 108, then answer the exam-style question below.

Paper ②

4. For this question, you need to refer to the **whole of source 13a** together with **source 13b**.
Compare how the two writers convey their different attitudes to parenting and education.
In your answer, you could:
• compare their different attitudes
• compare the methods they use to convey their attitudes
• support your ideas with quotations from both texts.

(16 marks)

When you tackle this type of question in the exam, remember to:
• spend about 20 minutes on your answer
• read the question carefully and highlight the main focus
• spend a couple of minutes planning your answer before you start writing
• always write about both texts throughout your answer
• identify the language and structural devices used and comment on how they help the writer to get across their ideas and arguments.

....

....

....

....

....

....

....

....

....

....

....

....

....

....

....

....

....

Remember: You have more space than this to answer your question in the exam. Use your own paper to finish your answer to the question above.

Writing questions: an overview

Both papers of the English Language GCSE include a writing section: Section B.

1 Read the statements below. Decide which paper each statement describes. Circle your choices.

   (a) The focus is descriptive writing.   **Paper 1 Paper 2**

   (b) The focus is writing to present a particular viewpoint.   **Paper 1 Paper 2**

   (c) It tests your ability to write for different purposes and audiences.   **Paper 1 Paper 2**

   (d) It tests your ability to write imaginatively and creatively.   **Paper 1 Paper 2**

   (e) You will have a choice of writing questions.   **Paper 1 Paper 2**

Assessment objective 5

(a) (Communicate) clearly, effectively and imaginatively, selecting and adapting tone, style and register for different forms, purposes and audiences

(b) (Organise) information and ideas, using structural and grammatical features to support coherence and cohesion of texts

---

Assessment objective 6

Use a range of (vocabulary) and sentence (structures) for clarity, purpose and effect, with accurate spelling and punctuation

---

2 Now read these statements below about the assessment objectives tested in the writing sections. Decide which assessment objective each statement describes. Circle your choices.

   (a) Tests whether you can communicate clearly, effectively and imaginatively.   **AO5 AO6 Both**

   (b) Tests how well you can use sentences and paragraphs to structure your writing effectively.

                                                                                    AO5 AO6 Both

   (c) Tests your vocabulary and whether you can use sentence structures for effect. **AO5 AO6 Both**

   (d) Tests your spelling and punctuation.   **AO5 AO6 Both**

   (e) Tests how well you can organise information and ideas.   **AO5 AO6 Both**

   (f) Tests your ability to write in different forms, and for different purposes and audiences.

                                                                                     AO5 AO6 Both

> **Guided**

3 Summarise each assessment objective into one short sentence without using the words that are circled in the descriptions above.

Assessment objective 5 (a) Write ....

....

Assessment objective 5 (b) Arrange ....

....

Assessment objective 6 Use ....

....

> Putting things into your own words and summarising ideas is a good revision technique. If you can summarise effectively, it shows that you fully understand what you are reading.

Writing questions: Paper 1

Paper 1 tests your creative prose writing skills.

1 Read the statements about Paper 1 below.
   Decide whether each statement is true or false.
   Circle your choices.

   (a) You need to write either a description
       or a narrative.   **True   False**

   (b) You can write a poem.   **True   False**

   (c) You can write a play.   **True   False**

   (d) There may be an image to write
       a description of.   **True   False**

> Turn to page 50 for a reminder about the assessment objectives.

2 (a) Which of the terms below is another word for 'narrative'? Circle your choices.

   | poem | description | story | conversation |

   (b) Define the term 'recount'.

   ....

   ....

3 Look at the exam-style question below. **You don't need to answer this question.** Instead, consider
   its form, purpose and audience and complete the table.

Paper ①

5. You are going to enter a creative writing competition. Your entry will be judged by adults.
   Either:
   Write a description suggested by the picture.

   Or:
   Write the opening part of a story about a climbing expedition.   **(40 marks)**

Form	
Purpose	
Audience	

Writing questions: Paper 2

Paper 2 tests your skills in writing to present a viewpoint.

1 When writing to present a viewpoint, you will need to write in a certain way. Circle the words that represent the writing form you should use.

| argue | inform | entertain | narrate | persuade | amuse | explain | recount |

Look at the Paper 2 exam-style question below. **You don't need to answer this question.** Instead, consider what it is asking you to do, then answer Question 2.

Paper ②

> **5.** 'There should be a curfew of 9 pm for all teenagers under 18, when they must return home.'
>
> Write an article for your local newspaper in which you explain your point of view on this statement.
> **(40 marks)**

2 (a) Circle the words in the exam-style question that tell you which audience you should be writing for.

(b) Circle the words in the exam-style question that tell you the form the answer should take.

(c) Circle the words in the exam-style question that tell you, or suggest to you, what the purpose of your writing should be.

Guided

3 Plan an answer for the exam-style Question 5. Consider who might be affected if a curfew is brought in. Write your notes in bullet points below:

• Teenagers ....

....

....

....

....

....

....

....

....

....

....

....

....

....

....

....

....

Writing questions: time management

The table below shows the three key stages to complete when answering a Paper 1 or a Paper 2 writing task.

Guided **1** Complete the table by writing in the number of minutes you should spend on each stage. The first row has been done for you.

Total time for Paper 1, Section B: Writing	45 minutes
Planning your answer	
Writing your answer	
Checking and proofreading your answer	

Total time for Paper 2, Section B: Writing	45 minutes
Planning your answer	
Writing your answer	
Checking and proofreading your answer	

2 Read the statements about the writing task below. Decide whether each statement is true or false and circle your choices.

(a) Keep writing till the end, even if it means finishing halfway through a sentence.   **True   False**

(b) Conclusions are important.   **True   False**

(c) Don't pause during the writing as you might lose marks.   **True   False**

(d) You should spend the same amount of time on Section A as on Section B.   **True   False**

(e) Use bullets to express your remaining ideas if you run out of time.   **True   False**

(f) Write a note to the examiner letting them know you have run out of time.   **True   False**

Guided **3** During the writing process, what are the six things that you can do to help you with time management? One has been completed for you

(a) Check I'm still writing in the correct form.

(b) ....

(c) ....

(d) ....

(e) ....

(f) ....

Writing for a purpose: creative 1

Look at the exam-style question below. **You don't need to answer this question now.** Instead, think about what you might include in a response to this title, then answer Questions 1 to 4.

> **Paper**
> **①**

> 5. You see a creative writing competition advertised. It is to write about a time when you visited a theme park.
>
> **(40 marks)**

Guided

1 Using the senses can help you to create a vivid picture in a reader's mind. Complete the table below to gather ideas you could use in your answer to the exam-style question above. Some ideas have been added for you.

At the theme park, I could...

see:	
hear:	
smell:	the sharp tang of diesel oil on the breeze
touch:	
taste:	syrupy sweet candy-floss

> When you describe feelings, try to use verbs that **show**, rather than **tell**, the reader. This will make your writing more engaging.

Guided

2 The exam-style question above encourages you to write in the first person. This means you can describe the narrator's feelings in detail. Finish this sentence about how you were feeling at the theme park:

My face lit up with a wide smile and ....
....
....

> Remember to keep the same narrative voice throughout your answer in the exam.

3 Figurative language will also help you to create strong descriptions and vivid images. For each of the following, write an imaginative example that you could use in a response to the exam-style question above.

Simile: ....

Metaphor: ....

Personification: ....

> Using fewer well-chosen words is more effective than using too many unimaginative ones.

4 Write the first three sentences of your answer to the exam-style question at the top of this page. Use your answers to Questions 1 to 3 in your writing. Remember to choose your vocabulary carefully and try to use verbs that show rather than tell your feelings.

....
....
....
....
....
....

Writing for a purpose: creative 2

Read the exam-style question below. **You don't need to answer this question**. Instead, think about what it is asking you to do, then read the opening section of one student's response and answer Question 1.

Paper ①

> **5.** You have decided to enter a creative writing competition. Your entry will be judged by people of your own age. Write the opening part of a story about a train journey. **(40 marks)**

1 Find examples of the narrative elements below. Annotate the student answer below.

(a) Narrative voice – is it in the first or third person?

(b) Engaging the reader – have they used any descriptive techniques: senses, feelings, language choice, figurative language?

(c) Structure – have they provided all the answers or offered hints of what might happen next?

> It was November and I was on my way to visit my grandmother. I was looking forward to the trip but the train was cold and I shivered as I pulled my warm coat tightly around me. The train started with a jolt, like a gun being fired. There was a woman sitting opposite me, knitting. She looked over at me and seemed cross.

2 What advice would you give this student to improve their answer?

....

....

....

....

....

....

....

3 Rewrite the student answer using your advice.

....

....

....

....

....

....

....

Writing for a purpose: viewpoint 1

Look at the exam-style question below. **You don't need to answer this question**. Instead, think about what you might include in a response to this title, then answer Questions 1 to 4.

Paper ②

> **5.** 'The internet is an addictive drug.'
>
> Write an article for a newspaper in which you explain your point of view on this statement.
>
> **(40 marks)**

1   Decide whether you want to write for or against the newspaper's suggestion in the exam-style question above. Then write down three key points to support your point of view.

Point 1: ....

Point 2: ....

Point 3: ....

2   Write down a piece of evidence to support each of the points in your answer to Question 1.

Evidence for point 1: ....

Evidence for point 2: ....

Evidence for point 3: ....

> Evidence could be facts or statistics, an expert opinion or an example from your personal experience. The evidence you use in your writing in the exam does not have to be real or true, but it must be believable.

Guided

3   A counter-argument allows you to dismiss an opposing point of view. Think about the points you made in Question 1 above. What opposing points might somebody on the other side of the argument make? How could you dismiss them? Write down your ideas.

Some people might feel ....

....

However, ...

....

4   Rhetorical devices can strengthen your argument. Choose one of the following devices and use it to rewrite one sentence of your answer to Question 3.

Some people might feel ....

....

However, ...

....

rhetorical questions	direct address	repetition	lists	alliteration
contrast	pattern of three	emotive language	hyperbole	

Writing for a purpose: viewpoint 2

Look at the exam-style question below. **You don't need to answer this question now**. Instead, think about what you might include in a response to this title, then answer Questions 1 to 3.

Paper
②

> 5. 'Libraries need to change to attract teenagers to use them.'
>
> Write an article for your school magazine explaining your point of view on this statement.
>
> **(40 marks)**

Guided

1   Writing that informs and explains often uses headings and subheadings to guide the reader and make the information easier to find. List up to four subheadings that you could use to organise your answer to the exam-style question. An example has been done for you.

(a) Social media

(b) ....

(c) ....

(d) ....

2   Using facts and statistics is an effective way to make your writing appear reliable. Write down four facts or statistics that you could include in your answer to the exam-style question.

(a) ....

(b) ....

(c) ....

(d) ....

3   Using the correct tone in your writing is very important. Texts that inform and explain usually have a formal tone as they need to sound trustworthy. Write the opening paragraph of your answer to the exam-style question above. Use a formal tone and try to use some of the facts and statistics from your answer to Question 2.

....

....

....

....

....

....

....

....

....

....

| Use adverbials to guide the reader through the information, e.g. first, then. | When writing to inform and explain, avoid using too much figurative language. |

Writing for an audience

Some Paper 2 writing questions will clearly state the audience you should write for. Others will only hint at the audience. Look at the exam-style question below. **You don't need to answer it.** Instead, think about what you might include in a response to this title, then answer Questions 1 and 2.

Paper
②

> 5. 'Technology is ruining teenagers' lives.' Write an article for your local newspaper giving your point of view on this statement. **(40 marks)**

> **Guided**

1 Describe the implied audience for this piece of writing. Include your thoughts on age and gender.

The audience is likely to be ....

....

....

2 Which of the following sentences has the most appropriate tone and vocabulary for the audience you identified in Question 1? Circle your choice, then write a sentence to explain it.

> A   Some teenagers spend half their lives gawping at laptops and the telly, which I reckon is just such a waste of time.

> B   When you see a teenager staring at a computer, do not assume they are wasting their time.

> Remember to think about how wide the implied audience might be. For example, although their main audience might be adults, newspapers are read by people of all ages.

....

....

....

Now look at this exam-style question. **You don't need to answer this question now.** Instead, think about the language you might use in your response, then answer Question 3.

Paper
②

> 5. 'To do well in your exams it helps to lead a healthy lifestyle.'
>
> Write a speech for Year 11 students, explaining your viewpoint on this statement. **(40 marks)**

> **Guided**

3 An answer to exam-style Question 5 has been started for you below. Add two sentences to this opening.

Let's get straight to the point. The whole 'eat your five-a-day' routine is boring. Especially when your parents hammer it home on a daily basis, and particularly when it's followed by the inevitable 'don't be a couch potato' speech. We don't always want to hear what's good for us. However, if what you really want is clear skin and to feel invigorated, then increasing the amount of green vegetables you eat is a good starting point.

....

....

....

....

Putting it into practice

Read the exam-style question below. **You don't need to answer this question**. Instead, think about the question options and what these might involve. Then answer Questions 1 and 2.

Paper ①

5. A local newspaper is running a creative writing competition. Your entry will be judged by a panel of teachers.

Either:

Write a description suggested by this picture:

Or:

Write the opening part of a story about hunting for treasure under the sea.

(40 marks)

> When you tackle this kind of question in the exam, remember to:
> • plan your time – you have 45 minutes for this question, including planning and checking
> • read the question carefully and decide which option to answer
> • plan your writing, including ideas about narrative or descriptive techniques you might use
> • make sure the form you choose is either a narrative or description
> • make sure you stick to the same narrative voice throughout your writing.

Guided

1 (a) Choose one of the options in the exam-style question above.

(b) Plan your time for your chosen option:

Planning time: .... minutes

Writing time: .... minutes

Checking time: .... minutes

(c) Plan your content for your chosen option. Complete the spider diagram below.

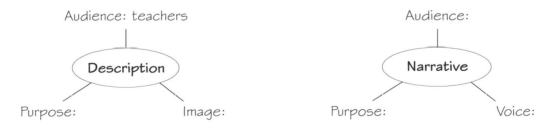

2 Note down some ideas about descriptive techniques you could use in your answer. Write a sentence giving an example of each technique.

Technique 1: ....

Example 1: ....

Technique 2: ....

Example 2: ....

....

Putting it into practice

Read the exam-style question below. **You don't need to answer it**. Instead, think about what it is asking you to do, then complete the table and/or spider diagram.

5. 'All dogs should be banned from parks.'

Write an article for your local newspaper in which you argue for or against this statement.

(40 marks)

> When you tackle this kind of question in the exam, remember to:
> • plan your time – you have 45 minutes to answer it, including planning and checking
> • read the question carefully
> • annotate the question to highlight the form, audience and purpose
> • plan your writing.

1 Plan a response to the exam-style question above by completing the table and/or spider diagram.

Timing	Plan: minutes Write: minutes Check: minutes	
Topic		
Form		
Audience		
Purpose		
Key features		

Form: articles

Read the Paper 2 exam-style question below. **You don't need to answer this question**. Instead, think about what it is asking you to do, then answer Questions 1 to 5.

Paper
2

5. 'There should be a curfew of 9 pm for all teenagers under 18, when they must return home.'

Write an article for your local newspaper in which you explain your point of view on this statement. **(40 marks)**

> Look back at page 52 to see the bullet points you wrote for this same exam-style question.

1 Think of a title you could use as a headline for this piece of writing.

....

....

> Headlines use a range of techniques including: repetition, a rhetorical question, alliteration, a pun or a rhyme.

2 Think of a subheading that will add more information to your headline.

....

....

3 Write your opening paragraph, summing up your ideas in two or three sentences.

....

....

....

....

> Remember that the quotations or evidence you use in your writing in the exam do not have to be real or true, but they must be believable.

4 Articles often use quotations from experts to make the information seem factual and reliable. Who could you quote in this article? What would they say?

....

....

....

....

5 Write your closing paragraph, concluding your article with your views on this statement.

....

....

....

....

Form: letters and reports

Read this Paper 2 exam-style question. **You don't need to answer this question.** Instead, think about what you might need to include in your response, then answer Question 1.

5. 'School uniforms are a waste of time.'

Write a letter to a national newspaper arguing for or against this statement.   **(40 marks)**

1 Decide whether the following statements are true or false. Circle your choices.

(a) You should make it clear that you are writing a letter, for example
   by using 'Dear…'.   **True   False**

(b) You should use 'Dear Sir/Madam' if you don't know the name of
   the person you are writing to.   **True   False**

(c) You should use 'Yours sincerely' if you have used 'Dear Sir/Madam'. **True   False**

(d) You should use a formal subject line to draw attention to your topic. **True   False**

> If you are asked to write a letter in the exam, pay attention to the tone and content of your writing.

Now read the following Paper 2 exam-style question. **You don't need to answer this question**. Instead, think about what might be needed for this piece of writing, then answer Questions 2 and 3.

5. 'Every local council should have a youth parliament.' Write a report for the council in which you explain your point of view on this statement.   **(40 marks)**

2 Reports need to be formal and factual. Write a headline and a suitable opening sentence for the report in exam-style Question 5 that give the main facts about the topic.

....

....

....

....

> Guided

3 Reports are intended to inform their audience about a particular topic, and usually include recommendations. Write two recommendations the council could use to attract young people to join the parliament.

(a) Firstly, I would suggest ....

....

....

(b) ....

....

....

Form: speeches

The techniques below are examples of what you could include to create an effective speech. Match the techniques with the example provided.

(a) Direct appeal to the listener	A 80% of students believe that homework is pointless and parents share this view too, with one mother commenting 'my child is so exhausted after 6 hours of school – they need to rest, not punish themselves till midnight!'
(b) Use of emotive language to effectively express ideas	B Children aren't machines – they are people. Children shouldn't be treated with little respect – they have a voice too.
(c) Range of facts and opinions to support opinion	C Social media may be a distraction for some, though it's been an invaluable tool for me to keep connected – especially when I'm at a low point.
(d) Addresses challenges and offers solutions	D The pain and anguish felt by animals who are neglected needs to be taken seriously.
(e) Uses repetition effectively to reinforce your viewpoint	E Take action and fight for democracy. Gain power through debate. Encourage others to join our cause.
(f) Use personal examples to illustrate your point of view	F Fellow students, I hope you share my concern for our future.
(g) Use of short, direct statements	G I can fully understand that funding will be an issue, though have you considered asking a local business to support my idea?
(h) Use rhetorical questions to encourage and provoke your listener to engage in the debate	H How can you sit there and let this injustice continue?

Read the Paper 2 exam-style question below and plan a speech. Use the guidance above to help with formulating your plan.

Paper ② 5. 'Celebrities deserve our criticism not admiration.' Write a speech for a youth group in which you explain your point of view on this statement.   **(40 marks)**

....

....

....

....

....

....

....

Putting it into practice

1 Answer the exam-style question below. Focus in particular on audience, purpose and form.

Paper
②

5. 'Students work hard all day at school, they should not have to do homework as well.'

Write a report for the chair of governors in which you argue for or against this
statement.   **(40 marks)**

> When you tackle this type of question in the exam, remember to:
> • read the question carefully and identify the topic, form, audience and purpose of the writing
> • plan your writing before you start
> • include all the relevant key features of the form and purpose
> • spend 45 minutes on your answer, including planning and checking time.

....
....
....
....
....
....
....
....
....
....
....
....
....
....
....
....
....
....
....
....

> **Remember:** You have more space than this to answer your question
> in the exam. Use your own paper to finish your answer to the
> question above.

Ideas and planning: creative

Read this exam-style question. **You don't need to answer this question**. Instead, consider the question options, then answer Questions 1 and 2.

Paper

5. Your local newspaper is running a creative writing competition. Your entry will be judged by students your own age.

Either:

Write a description suggested by this picture:

Or:

Write a story about a character who travels from the countryside to find work in the city.

(40 marks)

1 Write down your initial ideas for the description of the photograph option either as a list or a spider diagram.

> In the exam, choose an option quickly to save time for planning.

> Guided

2 Now look at a student's plan for the title 'Moving to a city', below. Add details to the plan, including ideas about creative writing techniques you could use.

> Try to picture the scene or event in your mind. Think about the characters (e.g. who is there, what they are like) and the action (e.g. what is happening, what has happened already).

Leaving family behind – moving to the city

Use adjectives to describe the sights and sounds of the city

Use five senses to describe highs and lows of life in the city

> Stay focused on the title you have chosen. After planning, quickly check that all your ideas are centred on this title.

Had a go ☐ **Nearly there** ☐ **Nailed it!** ☐

Structure: creative

It is important to structure your creative writing effectively. It is often best to use a narrative structure. Look at the exam-style question below. **You don't need to answer this question**. Instead, think about how you might structure an answer to this question, then answer Question 1 below.

Paper ①

5. Your youth club has organised a creative writing competition.

   Write a story about a character who returns home after a long time away. **(40 marks)**

> **Guided**

1 Complete the narrative structure for your story, entitled 'The Return'. Remember to include ideas about appropriate creative writing techniques in your plan.

> **Exposition:** Relaxing in front of fire on windy winter day. Doorbell rings.
>
> I answer – it is my long-lost sister. Use dialogue.

⬇

> **Complication:** . . . .
>
> . . . .

⬇

> **Crisis:** . . . .
>
> . . . .

⬇

> **Resolution:** . . . .
>
> . . . .

2 You can make a narrative more interesting, or tense, by playing with the narrative structure. Rewrite your plan in Question 1, this time starting at the crisis and using flashbacks to tell the story.

Crisis: ....

Exposition: ....

Complication: ....

Return to crisis: ....

Resolution: ....

Beginnings and endings: creative

The beginning of your creative writing needs to engage the reader immediately and set the tone for the rest of the narrative or recount.

Look at this exam-style question option. **You don't need to answer this question now.** Instead, think about how you might begin and end an answer to this question option, then answer Question 1 below.

Paper 1

> **5.** Your school magazine is asking for examples of creative writing for next month's edition.
>
> Write a story about a secret.   **(40 marks)**

> **Guided**

1 Write several different beginnings in response to exam-style Question 5.

> Don't be tempted to over-use dialogue. Mix it in with plenty of prose, to demonstrate your sentence structure skills.

Vivid description	Dialogue
	"I'm telling you, I saw her out there, clear as day!" hissed my aunt. "Ssh" whispered my father. "Just keep the secret until she's old enough to handle it!" Through the tiny crack in the door I could see my father's anguished face. My mind raced ahead imagining a million different scenarios, none of them happy. Could they really be talking about my long-lost mother?
Mystery	**Conflict or danger**

The ending of a piece of creative writing is just as important as the opening. Choose one of your openings from Question 1, then answer Questions 2 and 3.

2 What will the tone of your ending be? Will it be happy, tense or sad? Write a sentence explaining how you would end your story.

....

....

3 Write three possible final sentences. Make sure you focus on creating the tone you decided on in Question 2.

(a) ....

(b) ....

(c) ....

> Make your ending as imaginative as possible. Avoid clichés like 'and they all lived happily ever after'.

Putting it into practice

Read the exam-style question below. **You don't need to answer this question**. Instead, think about the title options then answer Question 1.

Paper ①

5. You see an advert for a creative writing competition. It is going to be judged by the town mayor.

Either:

Write a description suggested by this picture:

Or:

Write a short story about standing up for an issue.   **(40 marks)**

> When you plan for this type of question in the exam, remember to:
> • read each question option carefully
> • decide which question to answer
> • spend 5 minutes on a detailed plan
> • plan the narrative voice and creative writing techniques you will use.

1 Choose one of the question options from the exam-style question above. Then use the space below to plan your answer.

Ideas and planning: viewpoint 1

Read the exam-style question below. **You don't need to answer this question**. Instead, think about what it is asking you to do, then answer Question 1.

Paper ②

5. 'Exams should be scrapped because they do not give a fair and accurate picture of a student's real abilities.'

Write a letter to your MP in which you explain your point of view on this statement.　**(40 marks)**

1 Plan an answer to the exam-style question. Work through the planning stages and complete the spider diagram below.
  (a) Decide whether you agree or disagree with the point of view in the question. Summarise your response in the centre of the spider diagram below.
  (b) To guide readers, plan an introduction that tells them what you are writing and why they should read it. Add it to the spider diagram.
  (c) Decide on the **three** key points you will make.
  (d) Decide on the evidence you will use to support your key points.
  (e) Sequence your key points by numbering them. What would be the most logical or effective order?
  (f) Add a counter-argument to your plan. What might someone who opposed your opinion argue? How can you dismiss their argument?
  (g) Plan a conclusion that will reinforce your point of view.

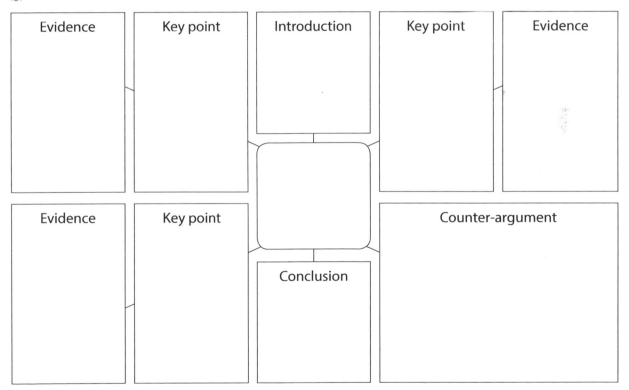

Remember:
* you only have **45 minutes** to plan, write and check this task – so aim for six paragraphs of well-crafted writing
* quality is rewarded – quantity is not.

Ideas and planning: viewpoint 2

Read the exam-style question below. **You don't need to answer this question**. Instead, think about what it is asking you to do, then answer Question 1.

Paper
②

5. 'The support given to Year 7 students is inadequate, making the transfer from primary to secondary school traumatic for some children.'

Write a report to the head of Year 7 in which you explain your point of view on this statement.

(40 marks)

> **Guided**   1   Plan an answer to the exam-style question. Work through the planning stages below and then complete the spider diagram. Some ideas have been added for you.

(a) Plan your introduction. Tell your reader what you are writing about and why it is important.

(b) You will need three or four key points. Decide which key points you will include.

(c) Add detailed ideas to each of your key points, including techniques appropriate to your audience and purpose.

(d) Number your key points. Which will work best at the beginning and which at the end?

(e) Plan your conclusion.

(f) Add ideas for temporal adverbials that would help to guide your reader through your points.

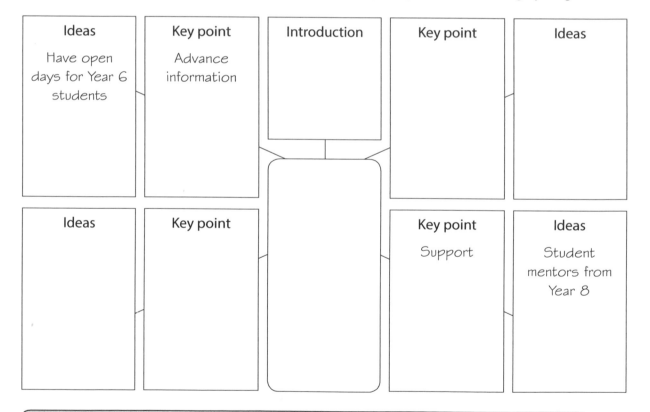

Ideas	Key point	Introduction	Key point	Ideas
Have open days for Year 6 students	Advance information			

Ideas	Key point		Key point	Ideas
			Support	Student mentors from Year 8

> **Remember**: You have 45 minutes to complete your writing of this question in the exam, including 5 minutes' planning and 5 minutes' checking time. Plan your writing carefully – quality is more important than quantity.

Openings: viewpoint

Read the exam-style question below. **You don't need to answer this question now**. Instead, think about what it is asking you to do, then answer Questions 1 and 2.

Paper
②

> 5 'Sending people to prison does not prevent serious crime.'
>
> Write an article for a national newspaper in which you explain your point of view
> on this statement.   **(40 marks)**

Guided 1 The first sentences of your writing must grab the reader's attention and make them want to read on. Try writing the opening sentence of your response to the exam-style question above in lots of different ways.

Using a rhetorical question: ....

....

Making a bold or controversial statement: ....

....

With a relevant quotation: ....

....

With a shocking or surprising fact or statistic: ....

....

With a short, relevant, interesting anecdote: My frail, elderly grandmother never recovered from a mugging. It happened in her own road, in broad daylight, in front of several dozen witnesses.

2 Choose one or two of your ideas from Question 1 and write the rest of your introduction to the exam-style question above. Remember your introduction needs to introduce:
   • the topic you are writing about
   • your argument.

....

....

....

....

....

....

Don't tell the reader what you are going to be writing in your article:

In this article I am going to argue that ...   ✗

Just write it!

Conclusions: viewpoint

Read the exam-style question below. **You don't need to answer this question now.** Instead, think about what it is asking you to do, then answer Questions 1 and 2.

Paper
②

> **5.** 'Sending people to prison does not prevent serious crime.'
>
> Write an article for a national newspaper in which you explain your point of view on this statement.
>
> (40 marks)

Guided

1 The final paragraph or conclusion of your writing should make a lasting impression. Try writing sentences you could include in your conclusion to the exam-style question above, using the techniques below.
An example has been done for you.

End on a vivid image: ....

....

End on a warning: ....

....

End on a happy note: ....

....

End on a thought-provoking question: How many vulnerable old people will be violently assaulted?

End on a 'call to action': ....

....

Refer back to your introduction, but don't repeat it: ....

....

2 Choose one or two of your ideas from Question 1 and write your conclusion to the exam-style question above.

....

....

....

....

....

....

....

....

....

....

....

> Look back over your whole argument. Consider how you might sum it up to end your piece of writing neatly and leave your reader with a clear message.

Putting it into practice

Read the exam-style question below. **You don't need to answer this question**. Instead, think about what you are being asked to do, then answer Question 1.

5. 'There should be a tax on sugar to pay for a government subsidy on fruit and vegetables to improve the nation's health.'

Write a letter to a national newspaper in which you argue for or against this statement.

(40 marks)

When you plan for this type of question in the exam, remember to:
- read the question carefully and identify the topic
- identify the form, audience and purpose before you start
- spend 5 minutes planning your answer
- note down the features and techniques you will use to support the form, audience and purpose
- organise and sequence your ideas
- plan your introduction and conclusion.

1 Use the space below to plan your answer to the exam-style question above.

Paragraphing

Look at this exam-style question.

Paper

5. 'There isn't enough careers advice given in schools.'

Write an article for your school magazine in which you explain your point of view on this statement.

(40 marks)

Read this student's response to the exam-style question, then answer Questions 1 to 4.

> When students choose their GCSE options in Year Nine, they do not always choose subjects because they will help them in their future career. I chose my GCSEs either because I liked the teacher or because lots of my friends had chosen that subject. Neither of these reasons is sound. With more advice on the careers available to us and the different ways we can prepare for them, students would make more informed and more sensible decisions.

This student has organised the paragraphs in her argument using Point–Evidence–Explain.

1 Identify and label the three different sections of this paragraph: **point**, **evidence** and **explain**.

2 Plan your own Point–Evidence–Explain paragraph in answer to the exam-style question above.

Point: ....

Evidence: ....

Explain: ....

3 Now write the paragraph you have planned in full.

....

....

....

....

....

....

....

....

....

4 Identify and label the three different sections of your paragraph: **point**, **evidence** and **explain**.

> Each time you start a new point, start a new paragraph. If you are writing to inform, explain or describe, start each paragraph with a topic sentence.

Linking ideas

Different adverbials have different purposes.

 1 Copy the adverbials below into the table, adding each one to the correct column.

Consequently	Furthermore...	In particular	Significantly
For example	However	In the same way	Similarly
For instance	On the other hand	Moreover...	Therefore

Adding an idea	Explaining	Illustrating	Emphasising	Comparing	Contrasting
		For example			

> Remember that time or temporal adverbials – such as afterwards, before, meanwhile – are very useful for indicating the passage of time in creative writing.

Read the exam-style question below. **You don't need to answer this question now**. Instead, think about what it is asking you to do, then answer Questions 2 and 3.

Paper ②

5. 'Exams should be scrapped because they do not give a fair and accurate picture of a student's real abilities.'

Write a letter to your MP in which you explain your point of view on this statement.   **(40 marks)**

2 Look at the paragraphs below. They are extracts from one student's response to the exam-style question above.
Fill in all of the gaps using appropriate adverbials.

> Many students are enormously successful in areas which exams do not or cannot assess. ...., one student at my school runs his own business designing websites for local companies. This is not something he has learned at school and .... his success will not be reflected in his exam results.

> ...., some students' success depends not on hard work but on natural ability. .... this has more impact on less academic students. One student, ..., might achieve an A grade with little or no hard work, while another might have worked solidly and consistently for years to achieve a 'C'.

3 Now write your own Point–Evidence–Explain paragraph in response to the exam-style question above. Remember to use a range of adverbials to guide the reader through your argument.

> Look back at your planning on page 69 to help you.

....

....

....

....

....

Had a go ☐   Nearly there ☐   Nailed it! ☐

Putting it into practice

1 Answer the exam-style question below. Focus in particular on your use of paragraphs and adverbials.

Paper
②

> 5. 'Improving existing cycle tracks and building more cycle tracks would benefit communities.'
>
> Write a report to your local council in which you argue for or against this statement.   **(40 marks)**

When you tackle any writing question in the exam, remember to:
• write in paragraphs
• plan one main point or idea per paragraph
• use P-E-E to structure your paragraphs
• organise and sequence your paragraphs
• use adverbials to link your paragraphs and guide your reader through your ideas.

....

....

....

....

....

....

....

....

....

....

....

....

....

....

....

....

....

....

Remember: You have more space than this to answer your question in the exam. Use your own paper to finish your answer to the question above.

Formality and standard English 1

1 Link the term with the correct definition.

Standard English	Slang	Colloquial language	Register

is language at its most informal, which can be described as non-standard and ungrammatical. It is often used within small social groups and can be considered offensive in some cases.

is the variety of language used for a particular purpose or in a particular social setting.

is informal language that is not rude, but would not be used in formal situations and is often used in speech.

is the very formal aspect of English that is held by many to be the 'correct' or 'accepted' way of communicating that is not influenced or affected by different variations in regional dialect.

A student has attempted the exam-style question below.

Paper 2

5. 'The behaviour of some teenagers is making life for residents on some housing estates unbearable.'

Write a letter to your MP in which you explain your point of view on this statement.   **(40 marks)**

To Steve,

You must be quite comfy in that posh house – away from all the clowns who live round are way – well try living next to a kid who spends his time kicking a ball against your fence. It's not good enough and you bella do something about it or things could get pretty tricky for you if you know what I mean.

2 (a) What advice would you provide to the student, based on their opening paragraph?

....

....

(b) Rewrite their paragraph in standard English, ensuring that the writing is matched to the purpose and audience.

....

....

....

....

....

3 Your friend has asked you to read over his work (below). He has been asked to write a lively article for a teen website on how to cope with exam stress. What advice would you give him on how to make the writing less formal?

Friends, colleagues and fellow students. I'd be grateful if you would take a minute to consider my twenty suggestions on how to beat exam stress:

....

....

....

....

Formality and standard English 2

Look at the two exam-style questions below, then answer the questions that follow.

Paper ② **A**

5. 'Computer games have no value. They encourage young people to spend hours wasting time that could be spent much more usefully.' Write a letter to the chair of governors of your school in which you explain your point of view on this statement. **(40 marks)**

Paper ② **B**

5. 'Computer games have no value. They encourage young people to spend hours wasting time that could be spent much more usefully.' Write an article for a teenage gaming website in which you explain your point of view on this statement. **(40 marks)**

1 Look at the sentences below. Which exam question would their tone be appropriate for? Label each sentence either 'A', 'B', or 'Both'.

> Formal and informal language, standard English, slang, humour and point of view can all affect the tone of your writing. Think about the audience you are writing for and make your choice.

Point of view: first or third person

> Many people think that computer games are designed to empty young people's minds and fill their time.

> I think computer games have a number of benefits for everyone, young or old.

Formal or informal

> It could be argued that some games not only improve the player's problem solving skills but, played collaboratively online, can also develop the ability to work in a team.

> It's only oldies and people who don't know their Xbox from their Wii that come up with this sort of argument.

Standard English or non-standard English

> What is wrong with switching off your brain and turning on your games console?

> There ain't nothing like a session on yer favourite shoot em up to chill you out.

2 Rewrite the following student answer using more formal language.

> Think about using more sophisticated vocabulary, replace colloquial expressions, use abstract nouns, use adverbials and use the passive voice.

What's the point of computer nerds slaving away thinking up crazy games for us to play on if we don't buy them? I sort of think we have got to move on and make has beens understand that for us teenagers, video games are part of our lives so they should give us a break.

....

....

....

....

Vocabulary for effect: synonyms

Synonyms are words with similar meanings. You can use them to avoid repetition and to add variety to your writing.

1 Look at the sentence below. Think of **at least two** synonyms for each circled word.

Synonyms for 'students':
1 ....
2 ....
3 ....

Synonyms for 'improve':
1 ....
2 ....
3 ....

Students can improve their learning by doing more revision.

Synonyms for 'learning':
1 ....
2 ....
3 ....

Synonyms for 'doing':
1 ....
2 ....
3 ....

> If you get stuck, use a thesaurus – but first TRY to use the large vocabulary that you already have in your head. Remember, you won't have access to a thesaurus in the exam.

Guided

2 Look at each of the words in the table below. Complete the table by adding at least two synonyms for each word. An example has been done for you.

embarrassed	upset	scream	moment	annoyed
humiliated ashamed mortified				

Look at the exam-style question title below. Think about what you might include in a response to this title, then answer Question 3.

Paper ①

5. Write the opening part of a story about an embarrassing moment.   **(40 marks)**

3 Write a paragraph in response to the exam-style question above. Use some of your vocabulary from Question 2 in your writing.

....

....

....

....

....

Vocabulary for effect: creative

1 Look at this description.

> The sun's glorious golden rays burst through my gleaming windows, sending shimmering sparkling beams of incandescence dancing around my walls.

Rewrite the above description in eight words or fewer. You could reuse some of the original vocabulary or use some of your own ideas.

....

....

2 Look again at your answer to Question 1. Compare your shorter sentence with the longer original version. Which do you prefer? Write a sentence explaining why.

....

....

....

Now look at the exam-style question below, then answer Questions 3 and 4.

Paper ①

> **5.** A national newspaper is inviting entries for a writing competition.
>
> Your entry will be judged by journalists.
>
> Describe a place you have enjoyed visiting. **(40 marks)**

3 Write two or three sentences in which you begin to describe what you consider to be a great place to visit.

....

....

....

....

....

....

4 Look again at your answer to Question 3. Have you included enough description? Or too much? Do you need to add more? Or should you cross some out?

5 Look again at your improved answer to Question 3. Circle three words that you think could be improved. Write down three synonyms for each word, then choose the most effective one.

....

....

....

Vocabulary for effect: viewpoint

Emotive words are important when you are writing to argue or persuade.

 Guided

1 Look at the sentences below. Rewrite them, using emotive language to add more impact.

> A   Animals in laboratories are often treated really badly and then put to sleep.

Animals in laboratories are frequently treated cruelly and then slaughtered.

> B   If we continue to use too many of the earth's resources, the world will not have enough food.

....

....

> C   Our lives are filled with computers. We may not like it but we cannot do much about it.

....

....

2 Look at this sentence:

> Some parents greeted the school's controversial plans with a ⟨cry⟩ of disapproval.

What would be the impact of replacing the circled word with either roar, howl or whimper?

(a) roar : ....

(b) howl : ....

(c) whimper : ....

Look at the exam-style question below. **You don't need to answer this question now**. Instead, think about what you might include in a response to this question, then answer Question 3.

Paper ②

5. 'People joining the army are selfish glory hunters, running away from responsibility.'

Write an article for a magazine in which you explain your point of view on this statement.   **(40 marks)**

3 Write two sentences in response to the exam-style question above. Aim to choose vocabulary for its impact and its connotations.

....

....

....

....

....

Language for different effects 1

You can add power and impact to your writing by using a range of language techniques.

Guided 1 Look at the extracts from students' writing below. Some are taken from a piece of creative writing, some from a piece of writing presenting a viewpoint. Connect the rhetorical devices to the extracts.

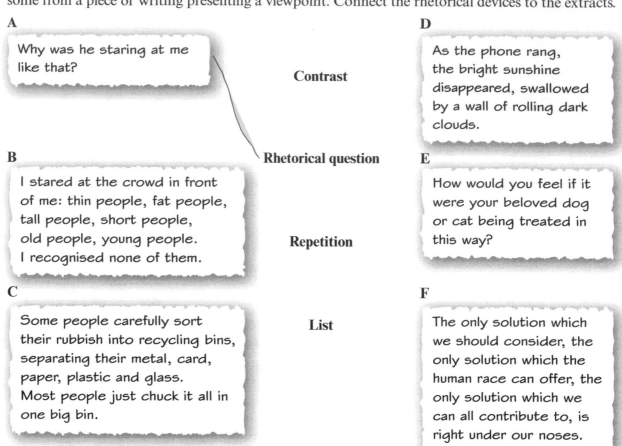

A

> Why was he staring at me like that?

B

> I stared at the crowd in front of me: thin people, fat people, tall people, short people, old people, young people. I recognised none of them.

C

> Some people carefully sort their rubbish into recycling bins, separating their metal, card, paper, plastic and glass. Most people just chuck it all in one big bin.

Contrast

Rhetorical question

Repetition

List

D

> As the phone rang, the bright sunshine disappeared, swallowed by a wall of rolling dark clouds.

E

> How would you feel if it were your beloved dog or cat being treated in this way?

F

> The only solution which we should consider, the only solution which the human race can offer, the only solution which we can all contribute to, is right under our noses.

Now look at the exam-style question below. **You don't need to answer this question now.** Instead, think about the language techniques you might use in a response, then answer Question 2.

Paper ②

5. 'Learner drivers should not be able to start driving until they are 21.'

Write an article for your local newspaper in which you argue for or against this statement.

(40 marks)

2 Use some or all of the language techniques explored in Question 1 to write four extracts which could be used in an answer to the exam-style question above.

....

....

....

....

....

....

....

Language for different effects 2

You can add power and impact to your writing by using a range of language techniques.

1 Look at the extracts from students' writing below. Some are taken from a piece of creative writing, some from a piece of writing presenting a viewpoint. Connect the rhetorical devices to the extracts in which they are used.

A

> For about the hundredth time that day, my sister started sobbing.

Direct address

D

> This is an appalling waste of money. We might as well be setting light to wads of ten pound notes and laughing as we do it.

Pattern of three

B

> How would you feel if it were your beloved dog or cat being treated in this way?

Alliteration

E

> We must act intelligently, decisively and immediately.

C

> The city stretched before me, dark, dangerous and disturbing.

Hyperbole

F

> Don't just sit there! Get off the sofa and do something.

Now look at the exam-style question below. **You don't need to answer this question now**. Instead, think about the language techniques you might use in a response, then answer Question 2.

Paper
②

> **5.** 'School is cruel'.
>
> Write a speech to give at an assembly arguing for or against this statement. **(40 marks)**

2 Use some or all of the language techniques explored in Question 1 to write four extracts which could be used in an answer to the exam-style question above.

....

....

....

....

....

....

....

....

....

....

Language for different effects 3

Figurative language can be used to create powerful images in the mind of a reader.

 Guided

1 Look at the examples of figurative language used in the sentences below. The writers have used similes, metaphors and personification to give their writing impact. But which sentence uses which technique? Circle the correct answer.

A The wind sang in the trees and the branches waved.
    simile   metaphor   personification

B The school has a challenging task ahead – an Everest to be climbed.
    simile   metaphor   personification

C She smiled like a tiger, licking its lips at the sight of a lost child.
    simile   metaphor   personification

D Waiting for the exams to begin is like waiting on death row.
    (simile)   metaphor   personification

E Homework is a ball and chain around every students' ankle.
    simile   metaphor   personification

F It's at that moment that your completely empty revision timetable creeps up behind you, taps you on the shoulder and asks if it could 'have a word'.
    simile   metaphor   personification

Now look at the exam-style question below. **You don't need to answer this question now**. Instead, think about the figurative language you might use in a response, then answer Question 2.

Paper ②

5. 'The school day should start at 10.30 am and finish at 5.30 pm.'

Write a letter to the school governors arguing for or against this statement. **(40 marks)**

2 Write up to four short extracts from an answer to the exam-style question above. Use one of the figurative devices explored in Question 1 in each extract.

....

....

....

....

Putting it into practice

1 Write a response to the exam-style question below. Focus in particular on your use of language and language techniques for effect.

Paper ①

5. You are going to enter a creative writing competition.

Your entry will be judged by students your own age.

Write a story about a locked room.   **(40 marks)**

....

....

....

....

....

....

....

....

....

....

....

....

....

....

....

....

....

....

....

....

....

....

....

....

....

....

Remember: You have more space than this to answer your question in the exam. Use your own paper to finish your answer to the question above.

Putting it into practice

1 Answer the exam-style question below. Focus in particular on your use of language and language techniques to present a viewpoint.

Paper ②

5. 'The tax on takeaway food should be doubled to encourage people to eat more healthily.'

Write a letter to your MP in which you explain your point of view on this statement.   **(40 marks)**

> When you tackle any writing question in the exam, you should think about language. Remember to:
> - annotate the question to highlight the form, audience and purpose
> - choose language that is appropriate for the audience and purpose
> - choose language techniques with care and for impact
> - avoid using too many techniques – it is more important that your writing is well structured and appropriate for the audience and purpose.

....
....
....
....
....
....
....
....
....
....
....
....
....
....
....
....
....
....
....
....

> **Remember:** You have more space than this to answer your question in the exam. Use your own paper to finish your answer to the question above.

Sentence variety 1

Using a range of different sentence types adds variety to your writing and helps to convey your ideas clearly and engage your reader.

> **Guided**

1 Look at the sentences below and identify the sentence type. Are they:

A a single-clause sentence

B a multi-clause sentence with a subordinate clause

C a multi-clause sentence with a coordinate clause

D a multi-clause sentence with a relative clause

E a minor sentence?

For each one, identify the sentence type by writing a letter in the space. Then write a sentence to explain how you know. One has been done for you.

(a) We must act now because soon it may be too late.

Type: .... Explanation: ....

(b) Surely not.

Type: .... Explanation: ....

(c) I hurried but I was too late.

Type: .... Explanation: ....

(d) He gave her an apple.

Type: .... Explanation: It has only one clause, with just one verb.

(e) The bus, which should have been there at half past ten, failed to arrive.

Type: .... Explanation: ....

Look at the exam-style question below. **You don't need to answer this question now**. First, think how you might use different sentence types in a response.

Paper ②

5. 'Sports people are poor role models as they are liars, cheats and fakes.'

Write a lively article for a newspaper arguing either for or against this statement.   **(40 marks)**

Now consider this extract from one student's answer to the exam-style question above, then answer Question 2.

> Professional footballers are possibly the worst 'fakers'. With just one tap from another player they fall over. Sometimes they dive to the ground. Occasionally they fly. They always start screaming. It shows they are seriously injured. They say it was a foul. They demand a free kick. It is ridiculous.

2 The extract from the student's answer uses only short, simple sentences. Rewrite the extract. Aim to use a variety of the five different sentence types.

....

....

....

....

....

Sentence variety 2

Look at the exam-style question below. **You don't need to answer this question now**. Instead, think about what you might include in a response, then answer Questions 1 and 2.

Paper ①

> **5.** Your school would like some examples of creative writing for its prospectus.
>
> Describe a character visiting a big city for the first time.   **(40 marks)**

Guided   **1** Write a sentence that you could use in your answer to the above exam-style question, beginning with the following. An example has been done for you.

(a) a pronoun (e.g. I, he, she, they): I grew up in a tiny village in the middle of nowhere.

(b) an article (e.g. a, an, the): ....
....

(c) a preposition (e.g. above, behind, between): ....
....

(d) an -ing word (or present participle) (e.g. running, hurrying, crawling): ....
....

(e) an adjective (e.g. slow, quiet, violent): ....
....

(f) an adverb (e.g. alarmingly, painfully, happily): ....
....

(g) a conjunction (e.g. if, although, because): ....
....

> Think about the first word of your sentences.
> Varying the first word adds interest to your writing.

2 Now write a paragraph in response to the above exam-style question. Aim to use:
- all seven different types of sentence opener in your writing
- a different word to start each of your sentences.

....
....
....
....
....
....
....
....
....
....
....

Sentences for different effects

> The ladder tipped over, the paint pot went flying, the paint exploded over her sofa, the paint pot hit her treasured vase, and the vase smashed into dust. I froze.

1 In the example above, a long sentence is followed by a short sentence. What effect is this intended to have on the reader?

....

....

> Guided

2 In the sentences below the same ideas have been used, but in a different order.

A   Before I walked the six miles home, I scrubbed every last drop of paint from the carpet and swept up every last crumb of glass, while she watched with a grim smile of quiet satisfaction on her lips.

B   While she watched with a grim smile of quiet satisfaction on her lips, I scrubbed every last drop of paint from the carpet and swept up every last crumb of glass before I walked the six miles home.

How does the order in which the information is organised affect each sentence's emphasis?

The first sentence emphasises ....

....

....

....

Look at the exam-style question below. **You don't need to answer this question now**. Instead, think about how you might begin an answer, then answer Question 3.

Paper ②

5. 'Donating money to charity is a waste of time, the money never reaches those who need it most.'

Write a speech for a Year 11 assembly arguing either for or against this statement.   **(40 marks)**

> Avoid overloading a sentence with too much information spread over a number of subordinate clauses. This can cause the reader to lose attention.

3 Write the opening two or three sentences of your own response to the exam-style question above. Aim to include a:
   • long sentence followed by a short sentence
   • sentence structured to give specific emphasis.

....

....

....

....

....

Putting it into practice

1 Answer the exam-style question below. Focus in particular on varying your sentences for effect.

5. 'All school students should be banned from bringing sugary drinks and snacks to school.'

Write an article to a national newspaper in which you explain your point of view on this statement.   **(40 marks)**

> When you tackle any writing question in the exam, you should think about sentence variety. Remember to:
> • use a range of sentence types
> • start your sentences in a range of different ways
> • structure your sentences for effect
> • avoid overloading individual sentences with too much information.

....

....

....

....

....

....

....

....

....

....

....

....

....

....

....

....

....

....

....

....

> **Remember:** You have more space than this to answer your question in the exam. Use your own paper to finish your answer to the question above.

Ending a sentence

Failing to use full stops, question marks, exclamation marks and capital letters correctly affects the quality of your writing.

1 When should you use a full stop? ....

2 When should you use a question mark? ....

> **Guided**

3 What three mistakes should you avoid when using exclamation marks? An example has been done for you.

   (a) You should avoid scattering exclamation marks randomly throughout your writing, and instead

   use them sparingly.

   (b) ....

   ....

   (c) ....

   ....

4 Look at the sentences below. Tick the two sentences that are punctuated correctly. Cross the one that is not.

   A I knew that what she had done was wrong, I had to persuade her to do something about it.

   B I knew that what she had done was wrong. I had to persuade her to do something about it.

   C I knew that what she had done was wrong and I had to persuade her to do something about it.

   > You do not use a comma to join two pieces of information in a sentence. Use a full stop to separate them or a conjunction to join them. So check every time you use a comma: should it be a comma or is the sentence complete?

   Now write a sentence explaining your decision. ....

   ....

   ....

5 Look at this student's writing. Correct all the full stop, question mark and exclamation mark errors you can find.

   ### A Change of Heart!!

   I braced myself for a confrontation, she was looking at me like she knew I had something to say and she didn't want to hear it. My heart began to race and a strange throbbing pain pulsed in my forehead. How could I say it. How could I tell her what I was thinking without upsetting her.

   She knew something was coming, tears were welling up in her dark brown eyes and her bottom lip was starting to quiver. I didn't feel much better than she did, my stomach was churning and I could feel my legs shaking. I tried to speak, my mouth felt like sandpaper, it was dry and rough and I couldn't form the words.

91

Commas

If you are confident with using commas, you will write more effective multi-clause sentences and lists.

Guided **1** Look at the sentences below. Some have used commas correctly. Some have not. Tick the correct sentences and cross the incorrect ones. Two have been done for you.

Commas in lists

✗ **A** They can comfort, us in a crisis help out when we're in trouble make us laugh or make us cry.

☐ **B** It doesn't matter whether they're tall, short, thin, fat, heart-stoppingly attractive or mirror-crackingly ugly.

☐ **C** She was loud, angry, obnoxious and painfully honest.

Commas in multi-clause sentences with subordinate clauses

✓ **D** Whether we like it or not, friends can hurt as well as help us.

☐ **E** Friends can hurt as well as help us whether we like it or not.

☐ **F** Although I had known her since primary school we never spoke again.

Commas in multi-clause sentences with relative clauses

☐ **G** The problem which we may not want to face, is that friends can sometimes let us down.

☐ **H** A friend who I will not name once told me all my worst faults.

☐ **I** Her house, which I only ever visited once, was enormous.

2 Look again at all the sentences in Question 1. Correct any that you marked as incorrect.

Look at the exam-style question below. **You don't need to answer this question now**. Instead, think about what you might include in a response, then answer Question 3.

Paper 1

5. Write a story about the perfect friend.   (40 marks)

> Remember to end your sentences correctly. Avoid using a comma splice.

3 Write three to five sentences in response to the exam-style question above. Use commas correctly to separate:
   • items in a list
   • a main and subordinate clause
   • a main and relative clause.

....

....

....

....

....

....

....

....

Apostrophes and speech punctuation

Make sure you know how to avoid the common errors of missing out or using incorrect apostrophes and speech punctuation.

1 Look at the sentences below. Some have used apostrophes correctly. Some have not. Tick the correct sentences and cross the incorrect ones.

Apostrophes in contractions

☐ **A** I do'nt see her very often.

☐ **B** I can't believe how things turned out.

☐ **C** She wouldnt answer the phone.

Apostrophes of possession

☐ **D** My teachers' face was a picture.

☐ **E** The school's reaction was incredible.

☐ **F** The boys' faces all lit up.

Speech punctuation

☐ **G** 'I don't believe it!' she shouted.

☐ **H** 'Never mind.'

☐ **I** 'Come over here.' he whispered.

2 Look again at all the sentences in Question 1. Correct any that you marked as incorrect.

> **Guided**

3 Now write a conversation between two friends in which they discuss a boy whose behaviour has resulted in several teachers ringing his parents. Aim to use apostrophes and speech marks correctly.

'Hey,' she called. 'Come over here.'

'What do you want?' I asked ....

....

....

....

....

....

....

....

....

> **Remember:**
> * apostrophes in contractions are used to replace **missing letters**
> * apostrophes of possession are always placed **at the end of the noun** whether it's plural (teachers') or singular (teacher's)
> * in dialogue, there is always a punctuation mark **before** the closing speech marks.

Colons, semi-colons, dashes, brackets and ellipses

Punctuation helps you to express yourself clearly. It can also help you to develop your ideas.

1 Look at the sentences below. How could you alter or add to the punctuation, using a colon or a semi-colon?

Colons and semi-colons

A There is only one thing you can do to improve your grades. Revise.

B Teachers can help. They can give revision tips and answer any questions you have about the exam.

C Revision isn't easy. It takes time and willpower.

D Exams are the problem. Revision is the solution.

> You can use a semi-colon to link two connected ideas instead of using a conjunction. You can use a colon to introduce:
> • a list
> • an example
> • an explanation.

Dashes and brackets

> **Guided**

2 Look at the sentences below. Some have used dashes and brackets correctly. Some have not. Tick the correct sentences and cross the incorrect ones. An example has been done for you.

☐ **A** My revision – which mainly involves staring into space – began this morning.

☐ **B** A short break (or sometimes a long break) helps clear your mind and recharge your battery.

☐ **C** My bedroom walls are covered in scribbled revision notes and key points (not a pretty sight.

☑ **D** Sometimes I wonder why I bother – and then I remember.

3 Look again at all the sentences in Question 2. Correct any that you marked as incorrect.

Look at the exam-style question below. **You don't need to answer this question now**. Instead, think about what you might include in a response, then answer Question 4.

> **Paper ①**
>
> **5.** Write about a time when you overcame a personal challenge.   **(40 marks)**

4 Write three to five sentences in response to the exam-style question above. Try to use:
   • a colon and a semi-colon
   • dashes, brackets and an ellipsis.

....

....

....

....

....

....

....

....

....

Putting it into practice

1 Answer one of the exam-style questions below. Focus in particular on punctuation.

5. Write a description suggested by this picture.　　　　　　**(40 marks)**

5. 'The price charged for top league football tickets is too high.'

Write an article for a sports magazine arguing for or against this statement.　　**(40 marks)**

> When you tackle any writing question in the exam, you should think about punctuation. Remember to:
> * use a range of punctuation accurately, including advanced punctuation such as colons and semi-colons
> * plan your time carefully so that you have time to check the accuracy of your punctuation.

....

....

....

....

....

....

....

....

....

....

....

....

....

....

> **Remember:** You have more space than this to answer your question in the exam. Use your own paper to finish your answer to the question above.

Had a go ☐ Nearly there ☐ Nailed it! ☐

Common spelling errors 1

Some of the most common spelling errors in students' writing are a result of misusing or confusing the following:

would of and would have

should of and should have

could of and could have

our and are

their , there and they're

affect and effect

words ending in ley and ly

its and it's

1 Identify and correct any spelling errors in these sentences.

A They went all the way back to there house.

B It would of been absolutley unbelievable – if I hadn't seen it with my own eyes.

C One affect of this issue is extremley concerning.

D Their first problem was how to get the students interested.

E Their our three reasons for this.

F There refusing to do anything about it.

G The school offered it's help immediately.

H We felt that students should definitley of been involved.

I Its not only the teachers who our effected by this situation.

J We were forced to reconsider are plan.

K It could not of been achieved without there help.

L Many students felt it had affected them negativley.

- There are very few words ending in **ley**.
- **Would of, could of** and **should of** are **always** incorrect.

M Its not the first time this has happened.

Common spelling errors 2

Some of the most common spelling errors in students' writing are a result of misusing or confusing the following:

| your | and | you're |

| of | and | off |

| two | , | too | and | to |

| whose | and | who's |

| we're | , | were | , | where | and | wear |

| passed | and | past |

1 Identify and correct any spelling errors in these sentences:

A He did not know were he was going or who's idea it was.

B To many people make the same mistake.

C The time for worrying has past.

D This has taken some of the pressure of us.

E Your never sure whether you're doing enough to help.

F Whose going to complain about that?

G We where the first people there but still they ignored us.

H They walked passed us as though we wear invisible.

I They went too far, taking it too an extreme.

J How can we tell who's to blame?

K It can be difficult to know when your in the wrong.

L Support for the idea soon began to fall of.

M We simply don't know whose argument to believe and whether were expected to agree or not.

> **Remember:**
> **A lot** is two words. 'Alot of people make this mistake' is wrong, but '**A lot** of people make this mistake' is correct.

97

Common spelling errors 3

Some of the most frequently misspelt words are explored in the table below. Make sure you learn how to spell these words properly.

argument	arguement	argumant
dificult	difficult	diffacult
disappoint	dissappoint	disapoint
disappear	dissappear	disapear
embarrassing	embarassing	embarasing
possesion	possession	posession
beggining	begining	beginning
recomend	recommend	reccomend
occassionaly	ocasionally	occasionally
definately	definitely	definitley
separately	seperately	seperatley
conscious	conshus	concsous
conshence	conscience	concsience
experiance	experance	experience
indapendance	independence	independance
beleive	believe	beleve
weird	wierd	weerd
business	busness	buisness
rythm	rhytm	rhythm
decision	desicion	desision
greatfull	grateful	greatful

1 Look carefully at the words in the table. In each row, one spelling is correct and two are incorrect. Tick the correct spelling and cross out the incorrect spellings.

> Correct spelling **can be learned**. Every time you spell a word incorrectly, make a note of the word and start to practise the correct spelling on a regular basis. Try strategies like looking for a hidden word within the word you are learning to spell, or saying what you see.

2 Now check your answers on page 134. Use the space below to write any spellings from the table above that you are unsure of. Practise them on a regular basis.

Proofreading

Proofreading is important. In the exam, plan your time carefully so you have time to check your work for errors.

1 Look at the extract from one student's writing below. Read it carefully, looking for any:
   - spelling errors
   - punctuation errors
   - grammatical errors – e.g. misused, repeated or missing words.

   Circle and correct all the errors you can find.

   > Scotland is the most amazing place Ive ever visited, even though it took ten hours to drive there it was worth it the moment i saw were we were staying. Huge blue lochs, rolling green hills, miles and miles of pine forest. They even looked beautiful driving passed them in a car.
   >
   > On the first day we took the dogs for a long walk through a forest, it was the quitest place Ive ever been. Even with my brother their, all you could hear was the sound of leafs rustling in the breeze, the birds singing and you're heart beating.
   >
   > Are hotel was great, the scottish people are so frendly. I would definitley stay there again.

2 Look back at three or four pieces of writing you have completed recently. How many errors can you find? In the table below, note down words which you have misspelled and the **kinds** of punctuation and grammatical errors you have made.

Spelling errors	Punctuation errors	Grammatical errors

> Train your proofreading brain to look out for the kinds of punctuation and grammatical errors you are prone to making. When the alarm rings, **stop!** Double check and correct any mistakes.

3 Use the space below to practise and learn all the spellings you have noted in the table.

Putting it into practice

1 Answer the exam-style question below. Focus in particular on proofreading your answer.

Paper ②

> **5.** 'Young people face many pressures.'
>
> Write a speech in which you explain your point of view on this statement. **(40 marks)**

> When you tackle any writing question in the exam, remember to:
> • save time after you have finished writing to check the accuracy of your writing
> • look out for the spelling, punctuation and grammatical errors that you know you tend to make.

....

....

....

....

....

....

....

....

....

....

....

....

....

....

....

....

....

....

....

....

....

....

....

> **Remember:** You have more space than this to answer your question in the exam. Use your own paper to finish your answer to the question above.

Cut along the dotted lines and staple the texts together to make your own
handy anthology. Make sure you keep it safe with your Workbook.

Source 8

This extract is from the opening of a novel by Aleksandr Solzhenitsyn and was written in 1962 but the action takes place in 1951. It follows a prisoner through one day of his long imprisonment in a Russian labour camp.

One Day in the Life of Ivan Denisovich

As usual, at five o'clock that morning reveille[1] was sounded by the blows of a hammer on a length of rail hanging up near the staff quarters. The intermittent sounds barely penetrated the window-panes on which the frost lay two fingers thick and then ended almost as soon as they'd begun. It was cold outside, and the camp-guard was reluctant to go on beating out the reveille for long.

5 The clanging ceased, but everything outside still looked like the middle of the night when Ivan Denisovich Shukhov got up to go to the bucket. It was pitch dark except for the yellow light cast on the window by three lamps – two in the outer zone, one inside the camp itself.

And no one came to unbolt the barrack-hut door; there was no sound of the barrack-orderlies[2] pushing a pole into place to lift the barrel of nightsoil and carry it out.

10 Shukhov never overslept reveille. He always got up at once, for the next ninety minutes, until they assembled for work, belonged to him, not to the authorities, and any old-timer could always earn a bit – by sewing a pair of over-mittens for someone out of old sleeve lining; or bringing some rich lag in the team his dry valenki[3] – right up to his bunk, so that he wouldn't have to stumble barefoot round the heap of boots looking for his own pair; or going the rounds of the store-huts, offering to be of service, sweeping up this or fetching that; or going to
15 the mess-hall to collect bowls from the tables and bring them stacked to the dishwashers – you're sure to be given something to eat there, though there were plenty of others at that game, more than plenty – and, what's worse, if you found a bowl with something left in it you could hardly resist licking it out. But Shukhov had never forgotten the words of his first team-leader, Kuziomin – a hard-bitten prisoner who had already been in for twelve years by 1943 – who told the newcomers, just in from the front, as they sat beside a fire in a desolate
20 cutting in the forest:

"Here, lads, we live by the law of the taiga. But even here people manage to live. D'you know who are the ones the camps finish off? Those who lick other men's left-overs, those who set store by the doctors, and those who peach[4] on their mates."

As for peachers, he was wrong there. Those people were sure to get through camp all right. Only, they were
25 saving their own skin at the expense of other people's blood.

Shukhov always arose at reveille. But this day he didn't. He had felt queer the evening before, feverish, with pains all over his body. He hadn't been able to get warm all through the night. Even in his sleep he had felt at one moment that he was getting seriously ill, at another that he was getting better. He had longed for the morning not to come.

30 But the morning came as usual.

Anyway, it wasn't surprising that he'd felt cold in the night. That ice on the window-panes! And the white cob-webs of hoar-frost[5] all along the huge hut where the walls joined the ceiling!

He didn't get up. He lay there in his bunk on the top tier, his head buried in a blanket and a coat, his two feet stuffed into one sleeve, with the end tucked under, of his wadded jacket. He couldn't see, but his ears told him
35 everything going on in the barrack-room and especially in the corner his team occupied. He heard the heavy tread of the orderlies carrying one of the big barrels of nightsoil along the passage outside. A light job, that was considered, a job for the infirm, but just you try and carry out the muck without spilling any. He heard some of the 75th slamming bunches of boots on to the floor from the drying-shed. Now their own lads were doing it (it was their own team's turn, too, to dry valenki). Tiurin, the team-leader, and his deputy Pavlo put on their
40 valenki, without a word but he heard their bunks creaking. Now Pavlo would be going off to the bread-stores and Tiurin to the staff quarters to see the P.P.D.[6].

Ah, but not simply to report as usual to the authorities who distributed the daily assignments. Shukhov remembered that this morning his fate hung in the balance: they wanted to shift the 104th from the building-shops to a new site, the 'Socialist Way of Life' settlement. It lay in open country covered with snow-drifts, and
45 before anything else could be done there they would have to dig pits and put up posts and attach barbed wire to them. Wire themselves in, so that they wouldn't run away. Only then would they start building.

There wouldn't be a warm corner for a whole month. Not a dog-kennel. And fires were out of the question. Where was the firewood to come from? Warm up with the work, that was your only salvation.

No wonder the team-leader looked so worried, that was his responsibility – to elbow some other team, some
50 bunch of clod-hoppers, into the assignment instead of the 104th. Of course he wouldn't get the authorities to agree if he turned up empty-handed. He'd have to take a pound of pork-fat to the senior official there, if not a couple of pounds.

There's never any harm in trying, so why not have a go at the sick-bay and get a few days off if you can? After all, he did feel as though every limb was out of joint.

1: Reveille: a military term for a signal to wake up
2: Barrack-orderlies: people responsible for tasks like cleaning
3: Valenki: knee-length boots for winter wear

4: Peach: to tell on someone
5: Hoar-frost: a type of frost
6: P.P.D.: Production Planning Department

Cut along the dotted lines and staple the texts together to make your own handy anthology. Make sure you keep it safe with your Workbook.

Source 9

This extract is from the opening of a novel by Ian McEwan. A couple are having a picnic when their meal is interrupted by a hot air balloon accident nearby.

Enduring Love

What we saw when we stood from our picnic was this: a huge grey balloon, the size of a house, the shape of a teardrop, had come down in the field. The pilot must have been halfway out of the passenger basket as it touched the ground. His leg had become entangled in a rope that was attached to an anchor. Now, as the wind gusted and pushed and lifted the balloon toward the escarpment[1], he was being half dragged, half carried across the field. In the basket
5   was a child, a boy of about ten. In a sudden lull, the man was on his feet, clutching at the basket, or at the boy. Then there was another gust, and the pilot was on his back, bumping over the rough ground, trying to dig his feet in for purchase or lunging for the anchor behind him in order to secure it in the earth. Even if he had been able, he would not have dared disentangle himself from the anchor rope. He needed his weight to keep the balloon on the ground, and the wind could have snatched the rope from his hands.

10   As I ran I heard him shouting at the boy, urging him to leap clear of the basket. But the boy was tossed from one side to another as the balloon lurched across the field. He regained his balance and got a leg over the edge of the basket. The balloon rose and fell, thumping into a hummock[2], and the boy dropped backward out of sight. Then he was up again, arms stretched out toward the man and shouting something in return – words or inarticulate fear, I couldn't tell.

I must have been a hundred yards away when the situation came under control. The wind had dropped; the man was
15   on his feet, bending over the anchor as he drove it into the ground. He had unlooped the rope from his leg. For some reason – complacency[3], exhaustion, or simply because he was doing what he was told – the boy remained where he was. The towering balloon wavered and tilted and tugged, but the beast was tamed. I slowed my pace, though I did not stop. As the man straightened, he saw us – or at least the farmworkers and me – and he waved us on. He still needed help, but I was glad to slow to a brisk walk. The farm labourers were also walking now. One of them was coughing
20   loudly. But the man with the car, John Logan, knew something we didn't and kept on running. As for Jed Parry, my view of him was blocked by the balloon that lay between us.

The wind renewed its rage in the treetops just before I felt its force on my back. Then it struck the balloon, which ceased its innocent, comical wagging and was suddenly stilled. Its only motion was a shimmer of strain that rippled out across its ridged surface as the contained energy accumulated[4]. It broke free, the anchor flew up in a spray of dirt,
25   and balloon and basket rose ten feet in the air. The boy was thrown back, out of sight. The pilot had the rope in his hands and was lifted two feet clear off the ground. If Logan had not reached him and taken hold of one of the many dangling lines, the balloon would have carried the boy away. Instead, both men were now being pulled across the field, and the farmworkers and I were running again.

I got there before them. When I took a rope, the basket was above head height. The boy inside it was screaming.
30   Despite the wind, I caught the smell of urine. Jed Parry was on a rope seconds after me, and the two farmworkers, Joseph Lacey and Toby Greene, caught hold just after him. Greene was having a coughing fit, but he kept his grip. The pilot was shouting instructions at us, but too frantically, and no one was listening. He had been struggling too long, and now he was exhausted and emotionally out of control. With five of us on the lines the balloon was secured. We simply had to keep steady on our feet and pull hand over hand to bring the basket down, and this, despite whatever
35   the pilot was shouting, was what we began to do.

By this time we were standing on the escarpment. The ground dropped away sharply at a gradient of about twenty-five percent and then levelled out into a gentle slope toward the bottom. In winter this is a favourite tobogganing spot for local kids. We were all talking at once. Two of us, myself and the motorist, wanted to walk the balloon away from the edge. Someone thought the priority was to get the boy out. Someone else was calling for the balloon to be pulled
40   down so that we could anchor it firmly. I saw no contradiction, for we could be pulling the balloon down as we moved back into the field. But the second opinion was prevailing. The pilot had a fourth idea, but no one knew or cared what it was.

I should make something clear. There may have been a vague communality of purpose, but we were never a team. There was no chance, no time. Coincidences of time and place, a predisposition[5] to help, had brought us together
45   under the balloon. No one was in charge – or everyone was, and we were in a shouting match. The pilot, red-faced, bawling, and sweating, we ignored. Incompetence came off him like heat. But we were beginning to bawl our own instructions too. I know that if I had been uncontested leader, the tragedy would not have happened. Later I heard some of the others say the same thing about themselves. But there was not time, no opportunity for force of character to show. Any leader, any firm plan, would have been preferable to none. No human society, from the hunter-gatherer
50   to the post-industrial, has come to the attention of anthropologists[6] that did not have its leaders and the led; and no emergency was ever dealt with effectively by democratic process.

1: Escarpment: a long, steep slope separating areas of land that are at different heights

2: Hummock: little hill

3: Complacency: smugness, satisfaction

4: Accumulated: built up

5: Predisposition: willingness, inclination

6: Anthropologists: people who study humankind

Cut along the dotted lines and staple the texts together to make your own handy anthology. Make sure you keep it safe with your Workbook.

Source 10

This extract is from a novel by Harper Lee. It is set in Alabama in the United States in the 1930s and the key themes of the novel include racism, and how good and evil can coexist.

To Kill a Mockingbird

The following Monday afternoon Jem and I climbed the steep front steps to Mrs Dubose's house and padded down the open hallway. Jem, armed with *Ivanhoe*[1] and full of superior knowledge, knocked at the second door on the left.

'Mrs Dubose?' he called.

5   Jessie opened the wood door and unlatched the screen door.

'Is that you Jem Finch?' she said. 'You got your sister with you. I don't know –'

'Let 'em both in, Jessie,' said Mrs Dubose. Jessie admitted us and went off to the kitchen.

An oppressive odour met us when we crossed the threshold, an odour I had met many times in rain-rotted grey houses where there are coal-oil lamps, water dippers[2], and unbleached domestic sheets. It always made me afraid,
10   expectant, watchful.

In the corner of the room was a brass bed, and in the bed was Mrs Dubose. I wondered if Jem's activities had put her there, and for a moment I felt sorry for her. She was lying under a pile of quilts and looked almost friendly.

There was a marble-topped washstand by her bed; on it were a glass with a teaspoon in it, a red ear syringe, a box of absorbent cotton, and a steel alarm clock standing on three tiny legs.

15   'So you brought that dirty little sister of yours, did you?' was her greeting.

Jem said quietly, 'My sister ain't dirty and I ain't scared of you,' although I noticed his knees shaking.

I was expecting a tirade[3], but all she said was, 'You may commence reading, Jeremy.'

Jem sat down in a cane-bottom chair and opened *Ivanhoe*. I pulled up another one and sat beside him.

'Come closer,' said Mrs Dubose. 'Come to the side of the bed.'

20   We moved our chairs forward. This was the nearest I had ever been to her, and the thing I wanted most to do was move my chair back again.

She was horrible. Her face was the colour of a dirty pillowcase, and the corners of her mouth glistened with wet, which inched like a glacier down the deep grooves enclosing her chin. Old-age liver spots dotted her cheeks, and her pale eyes had black pinpoint pupils. Her hands were knobbly and the cuticles were grown up over her
25   fingernails. Her bottom plate[4] was not in, and her upper lip protruded; from time to time she would draw her nether lip[5] to her upper plate and carry her chin with it. This made the wet move faster.

I didn't look any more than I had to. Jem re-opened *Ivanhoe* and began reading. I tried to keep up with him, but he read too fast. When Jem came to a word he didn't know, he skipped it, but Mrs Dubose would catch him and make him spell it out. Jem read for about twenty minutes, during which time I looked at the soot-stained
30   mantelpiece, out of the window, anywhere to keep from looking at her. As he read along, I noticed that Mrs Dubose's corrections grew fewer and farther between, that Jem had even left one sentence dangling in mid-air. She was not listening.

I looked towards the bed.

Something had happened to her. She lay on her back, with the quilts up to her chin. Only her head and shoulders
35   were visible. Her head moved slowly from side to side. From time to time she would open her mouth wide and I could see her tongue undulate[6] faintly. Cords of saliva would collect on her lips; she would draw them in, then open her mouth again. Her mouth seemed to have a private existence of its own. It worked separate and apart from the rest of her, out and in, like a clam hole[7] at low tide. Occasionally, it would say, 'Pt,' like some viscous[8] substance coming to a boil.

40   I pulled Jem's sleeve.

He looked at me, then at the bed. Her head made its regular sweep towards us, and Jem said, 'Mrs Dubose, are you all right?' She did not hear him.

The alarm clock went off and scared us stiff. A minute later, nerves still tingling, Jem and I were on the sidewalk headed for home. We did not run away, Jessie sent us: before the clock wound down she was in the room pushing
45   Jem and me out of it.

'Shoo,' she said, 'you all go home.'

Jem hesitated at the door.

'It's time for her medicine,' Jessie said. As the door swung shut behind us I saw Jessie walking quickly toward Mrs Dubose's bed.

1: *Ivanhoe*: a novel by Sir Walter Scott, first published in 1820
2: Water dippers: cups used to get water from buckets in households with no running water
3: Tirade: long, critical speech
4: Bottom plate/upper plate: false teeth
5: Nether lip: bottom lip
6: Undulate: move like a wave
7: Clam hole: the hole in the sand left by a clam (a sea creature with a shell in two parts, which can open and close)
8: Viscous: thick and sticky, between a solid and a liquid

Source 11

The science fiction novel by John Wyndham from which this extract is taken, tells of the rise of the triffids, an intelligent species of plant that is able to move.

The Day of the Triffids

The thing would be about four feet high then. There must have been plenty of them about, growing up quietly and inoffensively, with nobody taking any particular notice of them — at least it seemed so, for if the biological or botanical experts were excited over them, no news of their interest percolated[1] to the general public. And so the one in our garden continued its growth peacefully, as did thousands like it in neglected spots all over the world.

5 It was some little time later that the first one picked up its roots and walked.

That improbable achievement must, of course, have been known for some time in Russia, where it was doubtless classified as a state secret, but, as far as I have been able to confirm, its first occurrence in the outside world took place in Indo-China — which meant that people went on taking practically no notice. Indo-China was one of these regions from which such curious and unlikely yarns[2] might be expected to drift in, and frequently did — the kind of thing an

10 editor might conceivably[3] use if news were scarce and a touch of the "mysterious East" would liven the paper up a bit. But in any case the Indo-Chinese specimen can have had no great lead. Within a few weeks reports of walking plants were pouring in from Sumatra, Borneo, Belgian Congo, Colombia, Brazil, and most places in the neighbourhood of the equator.

This time they got into print, all right. But the much-handled stories, written up with that blend of cautiously defensive

15 frivolity[4] which the press habitually employed to cover themselves in matters regarding sea serpents, flying saucers, thought transference, and other irregular phenomena, prevented anyone from realizing that these accomplished plants at all resembled the quiet, respectable weed beside our rubbish heap. Not until the pictures began to appear did we realize that they were identical with it save in size.

The newsreelmen[5] were quickly off the mark. Possibly they got some good and interesting pictures for their trouble of

20 flying to outlandish places, but there was a current theory among cutters[6] that more than a few seconds of any one news subject — except a boxing match — could not fail to paralyze an audience with boredom. My first view, therefore, of a development which was to play such an important part in my future, as well as in so many other people's, was a glimpse sandwiched between a hula contest in Honolulu and the First Lady launching a battleship. (No, that is no anachronism[7]. They were still building them: even admirals have to live.) I was permitted to see a few triffids sway across

25 the screen to the kind of accompaniment supposed to be on the level of the great movie-going public:

"And now, folks, get a load of what our cameraman found in Ecuador. Vegetables on vacation! You've only seen this kind of thing after a party, but down in sunny Ecuador they see it any time — and no hangover to follow! Monster plants on the march! Say, now, that's given me a big idea! Maybe if we can educate our potatoes right we can fix it so they'll walk right into the pot. How'd that be, Momma?"

30 For the short time the scene was on I stared at it, fascinated. There was our mysterious rubbish-heap plant grown to a height of seven feet or more. There was no mistaking it — and it was "walking"!

The bole, which I now saw for the first time, was shaggy with little rootlet hairs. It would have been almost spherical but for three bluntly tapered projections extending from the lower part. Supported on these, the main body was lifted about a foot clear of the ground.

35 When it "walked" it moved rather like a man on crutches. Two of the blunt "legs" slid forward, then the whole thing lurched as the rear one drew almost level with them, then the two in front slid forward again. At each "step" the long stem whipped violently back and forth; it gave one a kind of seasick feeling to watch it. As a method of progress it looked both strenuous and clumsy — faintly reminiscent of young elephants at play. One felt that if it were to go on lurching for long in that fashion it would be bound to strip all its leaves if it did not actually break its stem.

40 Nevertheless, ungainly though it looked, it was contriving to cover the ground at something like an average walking pace.

That was about all I had time to see before the battleship launching began. It was not a lot, but it was enough to incite[8] an investigating spirit in a boy. For if that thing in Ecuador could do a trick like that, why not the one in our garden? Admittedly ours was a good deal smaller, but it did look the same....

45 About ten minutes after I got home I was digging round our triffid, carefully loosening the earth near it to encourage it to "walk."

Unfortunately there was an aspect of this self-propelled plant discovery which the newsreel people either had not experienced or had chosen for some reason of their own not to reveal. There was no warning, either. I was bending down, intent on clearing the earth without harming the plant, when something from nowhere hit me one terrific slam

50 and knocked me out....

I woke up to find myself in bed, with my mother, my father, and the doctor watching me anxiously. My head felt as if it were split open. I was aching all over, and, as I later discovered, one side of my face was decorated with a blotchy red raised weal[9]. The insistent questions as to how I came to be lying unconscious in the garden were quite useless; I had no faintest idea what it was that had hit me. And some little time passed before I learned that I must have been one of the

55 first persons in England to be stung by a triffid and get away with it. The triffid was, of course, immature. But before I had fully recovered my father had found out what had undoubtedly happened to me, and by the time I went into the garden again he had wreaked stern vengeance[10] on our triffid and disposed of the remains on a bonfire.

1: Percolated: filtered through

2: Yarns: long, rambling stories

3: Conceivably: possibly

4: Frivolity: silliness

5: Newsreel men: news cameraman

6: Cutters: editors

7: Anachronism: something belonging to another time

8: Incite: trigger

9: Weal: swollen mark

10: Wreaked stern vengeance: taken hard revenge

Cut along the dotted lines and staple the texts together to make your own handy anthology. Make sure you keep it safe with your Workbook.

SOURCES

Source 12a

> This extract is from *Cassell's Household Guide*, a practical guide to all aspects of life, written in 1869. This section explores the occupations available to women.

Occupations Accessible to Women: Elementary Teaching

THE great difficulty of the educational question in the present day, and the obstacle to complete success in the earnest efforts made, is the difficulty, almost impossibility, of finding sufficiently-qualified teachers. The demand created by the Education Acts is estimated at over 25,000 of both sexes – the women, however, being in the majority.

5 The demand at present in upper-class girls' schools, and in private families, for teachers holding some kind of certificate, is quite beyond all means of supply; and amateur teachers, with no guarantee for their powers, are quite a drug in the market[1]. Even the Government certificate, which represents the low, but thorough standard of attainment required for national schools, is much sought after; and it seems that, in future, the passing of some recognised form of examination, and

10 the possession of some kind of a certificate, will be essential to, and ensures the success or failure of every teacher's future prospects.

The demand Some hard study would, in some cases, be needed to supply the inaccuracy of the general style of a woman's knowledge as a very thorough grounding in elementary subjects is needful. Very few, even the most highly-educated of women, can work a sum in fractions or proportion[2] with rapidity,

15 much less explain every step of the process so clearly as to bring it within the comprehension of a class; and how few who write good English from habit can teach the rules of grammar correctly.

The school selected should be taught by a very good certificated master or mistress, where an assistant should be likely to learn the system of school drill[3] and discipline, and also how practically to manage children en masse[4], according to the latest approved Government rules.

20 The duties of teachers in elementary schools are both healthful and congenial[5]. The hours of work vary in some schools according to the season of the year, but usually the children assemble at 9:30 a.m. and are dismissed at 4:30 p.m. A quarter of an hour's run is allowed them at eleven, and an hour and a quarter (sometimes more) for dinner, thus reducing the actual school hours to five hours and a half. After school the hours are free for recreation, pleasant visits, or study.

25 From various authorities we find the average income of the certificated mistresses of girls' schools to be reckoned at £58, and of infant schools at £56 per annum. They live, in addition, rent free, and in some cases allowances are made for fuel, light, etc. Under the School Boards of large towns higher emoluments[6] are offered, £75 per annum having been fixed as the minimum salary for mistresses. The comfort and advantage of possessing a small home would render the position of an

30 elementary school-mistress an eminently tempting one to many a poor governess, could she but manage to qualify herself to hold the position.

1: **A drug in the market**: available in high numbers but no longer wanted
2: **Proportion**: work out ratios and proportions
3: **Drill**: practice, training
4: **En masse**: as a group
5: **Congenial**: pleasant
6: **Emoluments**: payments

Cut along the dotted lines and staple the texts together to make your own handy anthology. Make sure you keep it safe with your Workbook.

Source 12b

Michele Hanson explores the difficulties some teachers might face during their training. This article was published in *The Guardian* newspaper in 2006.

OK, you try teaching 13-year-olds

Shocking news: a young trainee languages teacher on placement at Tarleton High in Lancashire "lost it" in class, barricaded the door with furniture, trapping the pupils, and threatened to kill them with something nasty that she had in her handbag. But why shocking? Imagine yourself in her place, "teaching" about 30 13- or 14-year-old creatures. Do you have one or two in your house? Are they polite, quiet and cooperative? Or are they breathtakingly insolent[1], noisy, crabby, offensive, skulking, smoking, drugging, and whingeing that they are not suitably entertained? What if you had 30? Wouldn't you like something in your handbag to shut the little toads up?

I'm trying not to sound bitter here, but I have taught; I have known supply-teaching hell; and I, too, have blown my top, even though it was 3.30pm and nearly over, because by then they were still climbing up walls (really), throwing scissors, dribbling glue and screaming all the while ... and when that happens, sometimes one just cannot keep one's cool a second longer.

And 13 is a particularly cruel age. In my first year's teaching, I crashed the car and sliced my forehead open on the sun-visor. Back at school, with my unsightly 27-stitch scar, I passed two 13-year-old girls. "She looks uglier than ever," said they, laughing merrily.

To be a teacher, one must be calm, sensible, tough, smartly dressed ALL THE TIME, and attractive. Otherwise, you are done for. Any degree of sensitivity can be a handicap. I blame the parents, partly. They often think teacher is a child-minding serf[2] and their huge babies are innocent and truthful. A big mistake.

Now think of that young teacher. "She had been trying to get them to be quiet," we learn. So she had probably been shouted at and humiliated for 40 minutes. This was her very last day of several horrible weeks of a placement. The end of her torment was a whisker away, but, driven barmy by pupils, she still blew it. Her career is now ruined. But the children were "petrified ... burst into tears" and were offered "support". The pathetic little wets[3]. She was pretending, you fools – dredging up a last desperate ploy[4] to shut the monsters up. If she had cried, they would have laughed out loud. Hopefully, she won't be sacked. If that's what she really, really wants.

1: Insolent: rude and disrespectful
2: Serf: slave
3: Wets: feeble, pathetic people
4: Ploy: cunning plan

Cut along the dotted lines and staple the texts together to make your own handy anthology. Make sure you keep it safe with your Workbook.

Source 13a

In this extract Simon Carr describes his approach to bringing up his sons as a single parent.

The Boys Are Back in Town

The fact is, I run a pretty loose ship. There's a lot of give[1] in the structure. In our world of fuzzy logic and more-or-less, we need a lot of give to get by.

It hasn't been easy eliminating the details, but we've managed to work our way into a very light-handed regime: we found that the more rules we had the more crimes were created; petty
5 prosecutions started to clog up the machinery of life. Conversely, the fewer the rules we had, the nicer we were to each other.

Fewer rules, that's the important thing, fewer but bigger rules.

It is what I like to think of as a masculine quality, the theory of outer markers. The boys have very definite limits that they mustn't go beyond. Inside the perimeter they can do very much as they
10 please, but they must stay inside the boundaries. It's murky on the other side, they're frightened of the dark out there, I've had to see to that. But within the limits it's summertime and it's easy living. And that's what boys like – which is just as well because it's what fathers are good at: exercising a regime of benign[2] indifference and establishing outer markers their children mustn't go beyond.

15 Mothers tend to a different theory. They take a more active interest in the details and the way stations through the day. Mothers like a routine; they even say that children like a routine ('It gives them security'). This may be true, too, but in our house there aren't bedtimes, let alone baths before them.

The canon law[3] my boys operate to is listed here in no particular order. No interrupting adults. Of
20 course we like talking to children and we like them talking to us, but those demands for food, drink or attention that come in from nowhere, unasked, unexpected, they drive you nuts. Yes, and no swearing if you're a child not even words that sound like swearing. Except damn, of course, and hell. What else? As little stealing and lying as possible. No wanton[4] littering, no fighting except for fun or out of earshot. Be polite as much as possible – of course, you can't when you're
25 very angry. You must work hard at school. Screaming insanely, running round the house making absurd and disgusting noises, sliding in mud in the park after dark and throwing water bombs and tennis balls at windows – all these were encouraged.

But essentially, here was only one rule: they had to do what I told them. The advantage of this regime was obvious to them: I told them less – much less – than half of what two parents would
30 tell them to do. I had also taken President Hoover's remark seriously: 'My children always obey me. And the reason is that I find out what it is they want to do and then advise them very strongly to do it.'

Not surprisingly, respectable women have found it all very under-regulated. Something must be missing, they feel. Proper homes aren't like this. It's hard to understand how my boys can be so
35 nice without bath times. They can't understand why my boys do what they're told without complaining.

Even though their own children behave with much less respect, obedience, politeness, I feel an amused attitude to our household from a certain sort of other. When they're pleasant about us, I'm told, they call us 'free-range'. I haven't asked what they call us when not so well-disposed[5].
40 Perhaps we are 'semi-feral'[6], perhaps we are 'feral'. Perhaps they've looked through our hedges when we're playing a summer session of garden laser hunting.

1: **Give**: flexibility
2: **Benign**: kind
3: **Canon law**: the standards people are judged by
4: **Wanton**: shameless
5: **Well-disposed**: sympathetic, friendly
6: **Feral**: untamed, wild

Cut along the dotted lines and staple the texts together to make your own handy anthology. Make sure you keep it safe with your Workbook.

Source 13b

> This extract is from *Cassell's Household Guide*, a practical guide to all aspects of life, written in 1869. This section gives guidance on rearing children.

The Rearing and Management of Children: Moral Influence – Obedience

It is commonly believed that no harm can come of letting a child have its own way, so long as it is a mere babe. But this is a serious delusion. As soon as a child is of an age to express its wants, whether by one means or another, it is old enough to be brought into habits of obedience. Obedience is the first lesson to be taught and very sensible are all
5　well-managed babes of its meaning. No harsh words, no impatient gestures, need be added to enforce the rule, which consists simply in not doing as the babe demands, if it be not the right time and the proper place for the desired gratification[1].

Taking food as an example. If children were left to their own choice, they would be eating and drinking perpetually[2] of whatever came in their way, till the stomach could no longer
10　retain the improper substances. Wholesome food would be rejected for more palatable[3] sweets and dainties[4]. Before long, depraved[5] tastes would be confirmed. Much the same misfortune sometimes befalls over-fed children of the wealthy, notwithstanding[6] the care bestowed in other respects on their nurture[7]; and an impaired constitution[8] is the result. With respect to the time of feeding, irregularity should be guarded against, by not giving
15　children scraps to eat between meals; neither should they be exposed to the sight of tempting food at unsuitable times.

Another early opportunity of implanting a spirit of obedience will be found in the impulsive habit which little children have of seizing whatever they desire to possess. This habit requires great firmness in checking, and a determination on the parent's part to risk
20　a flood of tears rather than let the coveted[9] article remain in the child's possession. Added to the danger which results to little children from letting this habit of snatching have sway[10], the destruction of property is liable to be very great.

1: **Gratification**: satisfaction of a desire, indulgence
2: **Perpetually**: for ever
3: **Palatable**: tasty
4: **Dainties**: good things to eat
5: **Depraved**: wicked
6: **Notwithstanding**: regardless of, in spite of
7: **Nurture**: upbringing
8: **Impaired constitution**: poor state of health
9: **Coveted**: strongly desired
10: **Sway**: strong influence or control

Cut along the dotted lines and staple the texts together to make your own handy anthology. Make sure you keep it safe with your Workbook.

Source 14a

> John Arlidge reports from California on using electricity to control the mind. This article was published in the *Sunday Times* newspaper in 2014.

'Appy ever after

"Try to relax," says Isy Goldwasser. It should be easy. I've had seven hours' sleep, coffee and eggs for breakfast. It's 10am but it's already 27C. I'm sitting in a picture-book-pretty converted 19th-century opera house that now serves as Goldwasser's office at the centre of Los Gatos, one of the most prosperous towns in Silicon Valley[1]. The trouble is, Goldwasser has just attached two electrodes to my head and is about to start pumping electricity straight into my brain.

In the home of moonshots[2] and "anything goes" optimism, the serial entrepreneur[3] Goldwasser and his business partner, the neuroscientist[4] Dr Jamie Tyler, are the most off-the-chart business brains you'll find. "We'll soon launch a consumer electronics product that you can use to shift your state of mind," Goldwasser assures me as he hands me the machine that controls how much electricity flows from the electrodes through my skull.

You mean hack my brain to make me feel what I want to feel, rather than what I actually feel? I ask. "Yeah. We want to marry neuroscience and consumer electronics."

He hands me the controller. I select Calm mode. I turn the dial up and – Holy silicon mad professors! – it hurts. There's a sharp vibration that feels like the neurons[5] in my head are pogoing[6]. Not relaxing at all. I turn it down and wait. And then something remarkable happens. After a few minutes, I begin to slump in my chair, my pupils dilate and my breathing slows. I really do begin to feel more relaxed. I have another go for 20 minutes and the same thing happens.

"See!" says Goldwasser, not at all calmly. Next year Thync, Goldwasser and Tyler's company, will launch the consumer version of the product I'm testing. The two men won't go into detail because the design is still confidential. But the electrodes, which will come with a mini power pack, will be small enough to fit in the palm of your hand and be simple to attach to your head. They are likely to be controlled using a mobile phone app. You will use the app to select the mood you want to be in and determine how much current flows into your brain, using a simple slide bar. Two modes – moods – will be on offer first: calm and energy. More will follow. Thync is focusing on willpower, self-control, motivation, confidence and creativity.

Goldwasser believes harnessing willpower will have big implications in the treatment of obesity, alcoholism or gambling addiction…

Mankind has used mood-altering substances ever since we discovered alcohol, coffee and tobacco and later drugs, prescription or otherwise. Goldwasser and Tyler want to add that to the list of little helpers neuro-signalling algorithms[7], to give their brainwave technology its fancy name. Goldwasser, former president of the materials sciences company Symyx Technologies and Tyler, a professor at Arizona State University, argue that "unlocking the power of the mind – regulating[8] biology with technology – is the biggest new frontier of this century and will be one of the greatest advances of our lifetime. We're kicking it off."

Goldwasser and Tyler may sound bonkers, but if their timing is anything to go by, they're the smartest guys in the lab. Wearable gizmos are the hottest new sector in the trillion-pound global technology sector. Apple launches its first smartwatch in the new year and will be followed by wearable kit from Microsoft and Google, which promises new versions of its web-enabled spectacles, Google Glass. Many of the new devices are designed to improve our health by monitoring our blood pressure and our stress levels, keeping tabs on how much exercise we take and helping us to feel refreshed in the morning by waking us up as we are coming out of a period of deep sleep. Goldwasser and Tyler are taking the idea one step further, giving us the power to change the way we feel, whenever we want.

"Tap into your self-control. Tap into your creativity. Tap into your energy. Tap into your calm. Think of us as your third cup of coffee in the morning or your glass of wine at night," Goldwasser smiles.

1: Silicon Valley: an area in the United States, famous for its technology businesses
2: Moonshots: ambitious projects
3: Serial entrepreneur: someone who keeps setting up new businesses
4: Neuroscientist: a scientist specialising in the nervous system and the brain
5: Neurons: cells that transmit nerve signals
6: Pogoing: jumping up and down
7: Neuro-signalling algorithms: processes that signal nerve pathways
8: Regulating: controlling

Cut along the dotted lines and staple the texts together to make your own handy anthology. Make sure you keep it safe with your Workbook.

Source 14b

In this extract William James, a ground-breaking American philosopher and psychologist writes about the effects of hypnotism in his book *The Principles of Psychology*, published in 1890.

Victorian Hypnotism

Hallucinations[1] of all the senses and *delusions*[2] of every conceivable kind can be easily suggested to good subjects. You can make the subject think that he is freezing or burning, itching or covered with dirt, or wet; you can make him eat a potato for a peach, or drink a cup of vinegar for a glass of champagne; ammonia[3] will smell to him like cologne water[4]; a chair will be a lion, a broom-stick
5 a beautiful woman, a noise in the street will be an orchestral music, etc., etc., with no limit except your powers of invention and the patience of the lookers on. Illusions and hallucinations form the *pieces de résistance*[5] at public exhibitions. The comic effect is at its climax when it is successfully suggested to the subject that his personality is changed into that of a baby, of a street boy, of a young lady dressing for a party, of a stump orator[6], or of Napoleon the Great. He may even be
10 transformed into a beast, or an inanimate thing like a chair or a carpet, and in every case will act out all the details of the part with a sincerity and intensity seldom seen at the theatre. The excellence of the performance is in these cases the best reply to the suspicion that the subject may be shamming[7] – so skilful a shammer must long since have found his true function in life upon the stage. Hallucinations and histrionic[8] delusions generally go with a certain depth of the trance, and
15 are followed by complete forgetfulness. The subject awakens from them at the command of the operator with a sudden start of surprise, and may seem for a while a little dazed.

Real sensations may be abolished as well as false ones suggested. Legs and breasts may be amputated, children born, teeth extracted, in short the most painful experiences undergone, with no other anæsthetic than the hypnotizer's assurance that no pain shall be felt. Similarly morbid
20 pains may be annihilated, neuralgias[9], toothaches, rheumatisms cured. The sensation of hunger has thus been abolished, so that a patient took no nourishment for fourteen days. An interesting degree of the phenomenon is found in the case related by M. Binet of a subject to whom it was suggested that a certain M. C. was invisible. She still saw M. C., but saw him as a stranger, having lost the memory of his name and his existence. – Nothing is easier than to make subjects forget
25 their own name and condition in life. It is one of the suggestions which most promptly succeed, even with quite fresh ones. A systematized amnesia[10] of certain periods of one's life may also be suggested, the subject placed, for instance, where he was a decade ago with the intervening years obliterated from his mind.

1: Hallucinations: things (like sounds or smells) that seem real but don't actually exist
2: Delusions: false beliefs
3: Ammonia: a strong-smelling gas
4: Cologne water: eau de Cologne, perfume
5: Pieces de résistance: showpieces, most outstanding parts
6: Stump orator: someone who speaks passionately, in public, from a platform
7: Shamming: pretending
8: Histrionic: dramatic
9: Neuralgias: severe pains caused by nerve damage
10: Amnesia: loss of memory

Practice exam paper

The Practice Exam Paper has been written to help you practise what you have learned and may not be representative of a real exam paper.

In the exam, you will be given space to write in. Here, **you will need to use your own paper for your answers**.

GCSE ENGLISH LANGUAGE

Paper 1 Explorations in creative reading and writing

1 hour 45 minutes

Instructions
- Answer **all** questions.
- Use black ink or black ball-point pen.
- You must **not** use a dictionary.

Information
- The marks for questions are shown in brackets.
- The maximum mark of this paper is 80.
- There are 40 marks for **Section A** and 40 marks for **Section B**.
- You are reminded of the need for good English and clear presentation in your answers.
- You will be assessed on the quality of your **reading** in **Section A**.
- You will be assessed on the quality of your **writing** in **Section B**.

Advice
- You are advised to spend about 15 minutes reading through the source and all five questions you have to answer.
- You should make sure you leave sufficient time to check your answers.

Source A

This extract is from a novel by Susan Hill. Kingshaw is a schoolboy who has just found out he has to change schools. His new school is also attended by a boy called Hooper. Kingshaw knows Hooper and is frightened of him, so he has run away.

I'm the King of the Castle

Kingshaw walked forward very cautiously into the shed, smelling his way like an animal.

It was airless and very dark. When the door swung open, a scissor of daylight fell on to the concrete floor, showing clumps of trodden-down straw, and mud. Kingshaw took another step inside, looking anxiously round him. Nothing. Nobody. A pile of old sacks in one corner. He went slowly over to them and sat down. He was shivering a little.

Seconds later, the door slammed shut. Kingshaw leaped up and ran forward, but as he put his hand out to the door, he heard the click of the padlock. After that, silence.

For a moment or two, he waited. Then he said, 'Hooper?'

Silence.

10   'Look, I know it's you.'

Silence.

He raised his voice. 'I can get out of here, you needn't think I'm bothered if you've locked the stupid door. I know a way to get out any time I like.'

Silence.

15   If Hooper had locked him in, then he had been watching out of a window, and then followed him. He was cunning, he could do anything. Yet he had seen and heard nothing, and he had kept on looking back.

He thought, perhaps it isn't Hooper.

The allotment[1] led towards a thick hedge, and then into the fields. It was right away from the village,
20   there never seemed to be anyone up here. But now there might be. Last year, someone had been strangled to death twenty miles away. Hooper had told him that. Twenty miles wasn't far.

He imagined tramps and murderers, and the cowman at Barr Farm, with bad teeth and hands like raw red meat. Anybody might have been hanging about behind the shed, and locked him in. Later, they might come back.

25   Sometimes, they were not allowed to see the newspapers, at school, because of things like murder trial reports, but they had them all in the Senior Library, and Lower School boys got sent in there, on messages. If you began to read something, your eyes went on and on, you couldn't stop them until you knew every terrible thing about it, and then you had thoughts and nightmares, you could never return to the time of not-knowing.

30   He remembered that he was not going back to his own school. That was all finished. He went about the building in his mind, thinking about the smells inside all the rooms. Perhaps he didn't mind so much about the people, except for Devereux and Lynch. And Mr Gardner. People didn't matter. But he couldn't separate any part of it, now, it was the whole of his existence there, that jelled together in his mind, time and place and people, and the way he felt about them.

35   He was still standing by the door of the hut. Somebody had used it for animals, once. It smelled faintly of pig muck, and old, dried hen pellets[2]. The walls and roof were made of corrugated metal, bolted together. There was no window, no light at all from anywhere, except for a thin line beneath the door. Kingshaw put out his hands and began to grope his way slowly round until he came to the corner with the sacks. He sat down.

40   Perhaps they wouldn't wait until night before they came back. Anybody could walk down the allotment and into the shed, and never be seen. They could do anything to him, in here, choke him, or hit him with an axe, or hang him, or stab him, they could get a saw and saw off both his feet and then leave him to bleed. Kingshaw stuffed his fist in his mouth, in terror. Somebody had done that, he'd read it in one of the blood-bath books Ickden had had, last term. Ickden lent them out, at 2d[3].
45   for four days. Kingshaw had read it in the bogs[4], and wished that he could stop himself and dreaded the nights that came after.

Now, he said to himself, it's Hooper, it's Hooper, there's nobody else it could be. Hooper would be creeping through the grass, back up to the house. Then, he would just wait. Hours and hours, all day, maybe, wait until he decided it was time to let him out.

50   Kingshaw said aloud, 'I'm not scared of being by myself in the bloody dark.' His voice echoed.

But it was not the dark, only the thoughts which passed through his head, the pictures in front of his eyes. He remembered why he had come here, remembered Mr Hooper's face, smiling at him, that morning, over the breakfast table. 'You will be going to school with Edmund.' He knew nothing about the place, except its name. It was called Drummonds. They were the ones who knew.

55   The sacks at the bottom of the pile were damp, and now the damp was coming through. Kingshaw stood up. His jeans felt wet, over his behind. He went back towards the door, and lay down on his

side, trying to see out. But the crack was much thinner than he'd thought, now he got down to it, he could see nothing except a faint greyness. He stayed there, pressing his ear to the cold concrete floor of the hut, and straining for the sound of movement, for footsteps. There was nothing.

60 Then a few minutes later, the faint sound of a truck, going down the lane. Kingshaw leaped up, and began to pound and beat upon the door, and then on the corrugated walls, until they crashed and rang in his ears, to scream and yell to be let out, he thought oh God, God, God, please let somebody come, please let somebody come down the lane, or into the garden, please, Oh God, God, God, God…

65 He gave up. The palms of his hand were hot and throbbing and the skin had come off one of his knuckles. He sucked at the loose edge, tasting blood. Silence.

Hooper might have decided to leave him in the shed for ever. There was nothing and nobody who could stop him, nothing that he would not be capable of.

Eventually, Kingshaw crawled on his hands and knees back over the concrete and the mucky straw,
70 on to the sacks. He pulled out the bottom ones, which were the dampest, and started to spread the others over the floor. He meant to lie down. He could see nothing at all, only feel clumsily at what he was doing. Then, something ran out of the sacks over his hands. He screamed and began to beat them desperately against his trousers, terrified of what it might be. In the end, he was certain that it had gone. His fingers, when he opened them out again, were slimy and sticky.

1: allotment: a rented piece of land for growing vegetables or flowers

2: hen pellets: hen food

3: 2d.: two pence, in old English money

4: bogs: toilets

Section A: Reading

Answer **all** the questions in this section.

You are advised to spend about 45 minutes on this section.

1. Read again the first part of the source, **lines 1 to 5**.

   List **four** things from this part of the text that we learn about the shed.

   (4 marks)

2. Look in detail at this extract from **lines 6 to 18** of the source.

   How does the writer use language here to describe Kingshaw's feelings?

   You could include the writer's choice of:

   - words and phrases
   - language features and techniques
   - sentence forms.

   (8 marks)

3. You now need to think about the **whole** of the **source**.

   How has the writer structured the text to interest you as a reader?

   You could write about:

   - what the writer focuses your attention on at the beginning
   - how and why the writer changes this focus as the source develops
   - any other structural features that interest you.

   (8 marks)

4. Focus this part of your answer on the second part of the source, **from line 35 to the end**.

   A student, having read this section of the text, said: "The presentation of Kingshaw as a coward stops me feeling any sympathy for him."

   To what extent do you agree?

   In your response, you could:

   - write about your own impressions of Kingshaw
   - evaluate how the writer has created these impressions
   - support your opinions with quotations from the text.

   (20 marks)

Section B: Writing

You are advised to spend about 45 minutes on this section.

Write in full sentences.

You are reminded of the need to plan your answer.

You should leave enough time to check your work at the end.

5. Your school or college is asking students to contribute some creative writing for its website.

Either:

Write a description suggested by this picture:

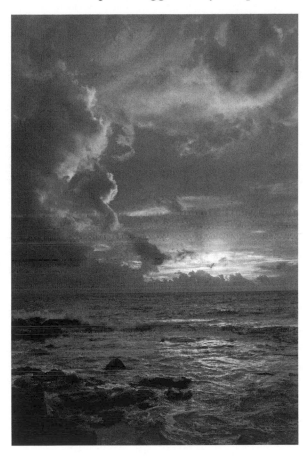

Or:

Describe an occasion when you felt threatened by your surroundings. Focus on the thoughts and feelings you had at that time.

(24 marks are awarded for content and organisation
16 marks are awarded for technical accuracy)

(40 marks)

Practice exam paper

> The Practice Exam Paper has been written to help you practise what you have learned and may not be representative of a real exam paper.
>
> In the exam, you will be given space to write in. Here, **you will need to use your own paper for your answers.**

GCSE ENGLISH LANGUAGE

Paper 2 Writers' viewpoints and perspectives

1 hour 45 minutes

Materials

For this paper you must have:
• **Sources A** and **B**

Instructions
• Answer **all** questions.
• Use black ink or black ball-point pen.
• You must **not** use a dictionary.

Information
• The marks for questions are shown in brackets.
• The maximum mark for this paper is 80.
• There are 40 marks for **Section A** and 40 marks for **Section B**.
• You are reminded of the need for good English and clear presentation in your answers.
• You will be assessed on your **reading** in **Section A**.
• You will be assessed on the quality of your **writing** in **Section B**.

Advice
• You are advised to spend about 15 minutes reading through the source and all five of the questions you have to answer.
• You should make sure you leave sufficient time to check your answers.

> Before answering the questions, read through sources A and B on pages 119 and 120.

Section A: Reading

Answer **all** the questions in this section

You are advised to spend about 45 minutes on this section.

1. Read again **source A**, from lines 1 to 18.

Choose **four** statements below which are TRUE.

- Shade the boxes of the ones that you think are true.
- Choose a maximum of four statements.

A   Aron kept himself alive by dislodging a boulder.   ☐

B   Aron had been travelling for six days before the accident.   ☐

C   The boulder was 800lb.   ☐

D   Danny Boyle helped to rescue Aron.   ☐

E   Aron didn't have a mobile phone.   ☐

F   Aron had two chunks of chocolate left.   ☐

G   No one knew where Aron was.   ☐

H   Aron had been climbing in Utah.   ☐

(4 marks)

2. You need to refer to **source A** and **source B** for this question.

Use details from **both** sources. Write a summary of the differences between the experiences of Aron Ralston and Sir James Clarke Ross.

(8 marks)

3. You now need to refer **only** to **source B**.

How does the narrator use language to create excitement for the reader in his voyage?

(12 marks)

4. For this question, you need to refer to the **whole of source A** together with **source B**.

Compare how the two writers convey their different feelings towards the disaster they face.

In your answer, you could:

- compare their different feelings
- compare the methods they use to convey their feelings
- support your ideas with quotations from both texts.

(16 marks)

Section B: Writing

You are advised to spend about 45 minutes on this section.

Write in full sentences.

You are reminded of the need to plan your answer.

You should leave enough time to check your work at the end.

5. 'People who engage in dangerous explorations should be criticised for their selfish actions, rather than being admired for their bravery.'

Write an article for your school magazine in which you argue for or against this statement.

(24 marks are awarded for content and organisation
16 marks are awarded for technical accuracy)

(40 marks)

Source A

Danny Boyle's new film, *127 Hours*, tells how climber Aron Ralston found himself trapped alone in a canyon and had to perform DIY surgery to save his life.

The extraordinary story behind Danny Boyle's 127 Hours

For six days, Aron Ralston kept himself alive with fierce self-control and a conviction that only logical thought could let him survive. But the epiphany when the 27-year-old climber realised how he could save his own life came from an explosion of blind rage.

Ralston had been climbing the narrow canyons of Utah alone when a dislodged boulder fell on to his right arm, trapping him against a rock. He was entombed in the wilderness of Bluejohn Canyon, carrying a small rucksack with just one litre of water, two burritos and a few chunks of chocolate. He had headphones and a video camera but no mobile phone – and there was no reception anyway. Most foolishly of all, he had not told anyone where he was going. He eked out his water, futilely chipping away at the 800lb rock and slowly entering a state of delirium, until he was eventually forced to cut off his trapped arm, with the small knife from his cheap multitool kit.

When his blunt knife pierced his skin but came to rest against solid bone, Ralston thought there was no chance he could perform the gruesome amputation that would save his life. He brushed some grit from his trapped thumb and a sliver of flesh peeled off "like the skin of boiled milk", he remembers. "I'm like, what the . . . ? I take my knife and I'm poking a bit more and the knife just slips into the meat of my thumb like it's going into room-temperature butter. My hand has almost jellified. The knife tip goes in and, 'pssstt', the gases from decomposition escape and there's this putrid smell. I go into this rage. I'm in this hyper-emotional state after all this regimented discipline to keep it together and in this moment, when I'm trying to rip my arm out from the rock, I feel it bend and it stops me – 'That's it! I can use the boulder to break my bones!'"

The year before his accident, Ralston quit his job as an engineer with Intel to climb all Colorado's "fourteeners" – its peaks over 14,000ft. In May 2003, he began "canyoneering" in Utah, navigating the narrow passages of Bluejohn with a mixture of free-climbing, daring jumps and climbing with ropes. He was negotiating a 10ft drop in a 3ft-wide canyon listening to his favourite band, Fish, when he dislodged a boulder he thought was stable. "I go from being out on a lark in a beautiful place and just being so happy and carefree to, like, oh shit. I fell a few feet, in slow motion, I look up and the boulder is coming and I put my hands up and try to push myself away and it collides and crushes my right hand." Ralston was pinned in the canyon, his right hand and lower arm crushed by the 800lb rock. "There was this stunned moment of what-?" he laughs. "And it's almost comic."

The next second, the pain struck. "If you've ever crushed your finger in a door accidentally," he says, this was "times 100". In an "adrenalised rage", for 45 minutes he "cursed like a pirate". Then he reached for his water bottle. As he drank, he had to force himself to stop. "I realise this water is the only thing that's going to keep myself alive," he says. Having failed to tell anyone where he was going, he knew he would not be found. "I put the lid back on the water bottle and gathered myself. It was like, all right, brute force isn't going to do it. This is the stop-think-observe-plan phase of rational problem-solving. I have to think my way out of here." As he describes how he thought through his options, he taps his prosthetic arm on his fingers.

He ruled out the most drastic option – suicide – but the next most drastic alternative came to him immediately. "There's this surreal conversation with myself. 'Aron, you're gonna have to cut your arm off.' 'I don't want to cut my arm off!' 'Dude, you're gonna have to cut your arm off.' I said it to myself. That little back-and-forth. Then, 'Wait a minute. Stop. I'm not talking to myself. That's just crazy. You're not talking to yourself, Aron.' Except I would continue to talk to myself in various ways, to remind myself not to pass out."

After two days spent fruitlessly chipping away at the rock with his knife and devising a clever but futile system of pulleys with his climbing clips and ropes to hoist the boulder clear – he was defeated because climbing rope is stretchy and he couldn't obtain the required tension – he put his knife to his arm, only to find it was so blunt he couldn't even cut his body hair.

The next morning, finally, came the rage and its revelation – that Ralston could fling himself against the boulder to break his own bones. From then, it was easy. The snap of his bones "like, pow!" was a horrifying sound "but to me it was euphoric", he recalls. "The detachment had already happened in my mind – it's rubbish, it's going to kill you, get rid of it Aron. It's an 'it'. It's no longer my arm. As I picked up the knife, I was very cool and collected." It took him an hour to hack through his flesh. "As painful as it all was, the momentum of the euphoria was driving it," he says.

Patrick Barkham

The Guardian, 15 December 2010

Source B

This extract is from a diary entry written in 1840 by a captain of a ship.

A Voyage of Discovery and Research in the Southern and Antarctic Regions

July 1840
During the night the wind and sea subsided, and we had a comparatively fine morning. We were all anxiously looking out for the Terror*, and wondering how she had weathered the breeze, when a wooden hoop of a cask was seen close to us. By this we felt certain that she had run past us during the time that we were hove-to for her, and was now probably far (5) *ahead; we therefore pressed all sail on the ship to endeavour to overtake her. The day being very favourable, we seized the opportunity of drying our sails and clothes, which had been most thoroughly drenched, and of repairing the damages we had sustained.*

In this and many other respects we felt the fine weather to be a great advantage to us; but this (10) *afternoon it pleased God to visit us by an unlooked-for calamity, – Mr. Roberts, the boatswain, whilst engaged about the rigging, fell overboard and was drowned. The life-buoy was instantly let go, and two boats lowered down; they reached the spot where we saw him sink only a few seconds too late! The gloom which the loss of one of our small party, at the outset of our voyage, occasioned, was for a time merged in feelings of painful anxiety, and afterwards of heartfelt* (15) *gratitude, for the merciful preservation of the whole crew of one of the boats, who in their humane endeavours to save the life of our unfortunate shipmate, very nearly sacrificed their own. Mr. Oakley, mate, and Mr. Abernethy, the gunner, had returned to the ship with one boat, when the other, still at a considerable distance from us, was struck by a sea, which washed four of the crew out of her. Mr. Abernethy immediately again pushed off from the ship, and* (20) *succeeded in saving them from their perilous situation, completely benumbed and stupefied with the cold. The boats were, with much difficulty, owing to the sea that was running, hoisted up, and not until after one of them had been again swamped alongside.*

We resumed our course under all sail, although this calamitous detention of some hours frustrated all our expectations of overtaking the Terror. A small iceberg, seen at a (25) *considerable distance just before dark, warned us to be vigilant during the night, which at this season being fifteen hours long obliged us to run at all hazards, or to delay our voyage to a ruinous extent. It has at all times a good effect upon those whose duty it is to look out, and an advantageous stimulus even to the most diligent, occasionally to see real dangers; but they were, in this instance, the cause of several false alarms, from the impression left upon* (30) *our minds.*

July 31
The weather continued fine all night and the greater part of the next day. Numerous birds of the petrel kind, which were flying about, seemed to enjoy the short-lived tranquillity, and were eagerly employed searching the patches of floating sea-weed for small fish and marine insects, (35) *which find a precarious security amongst its densely interwoven branches from the persecutions of their enemies.*

*The Terror – another ship.

Captain Sir James Clark Ross

Answers

Section A: Reading

1. The exam papers explained

1 (a) Paper 2
   (b) Paper 1, Section B
   (c) Read the extracts and make relevant notes
   (d) Yes – for Paper 1, Section B there are a choice of two writing questions
   (e) 10
   (f) To check through your work.
2 C, F have ticks
3 Complete the table with your own examples

2. Planning your exam time

1 A – 2
   B – 5
   C – 3
   D – 1
   E – 4

2

Paper 1		Marks allocated	Time I should spend
	Reading time		15 minutes
Section A: Reading	Q1	4	5 minutes
	Q2	8	10 minutes
	Q3	8	10 minutes
	Q4	20	20 minutes
Section B: Writing	Planning time		5 minutes
	Q5	40	35 minutes
	Checking my answers		5 minutes
	Total time:		1 hour and 45 minutes

Paper 2		Marks allocated	Time I should spend
	Reading time		15 minutes
Section A: Reading	Q1	4	5 minutes
	Q2	8	8 minutes
	Q3	12	12 minutes
	Q4	16	20 minutes
Section B: Writing	Planning time		5 minutes
	Q5	40	35 minutes
	Checking my answers		5 minutes
	Total time:		1 hour and 45 minutes

3. Paper 1 Reading questions 1

1 AO1(a)
2 (a) language/children's fear/Mrs Dubose
   (b) 10 minutes
3 (a) A02
   (b) A01(a)

4. Paper 1 Reading questions 2

1 C, D, E, G
2 B, D, E, F

5. Paper 2 Reading questions 1

1 (a) A2
   (b) 5 minutes
   (c) 8 minutes
   (d) A1
   (e) You shade in the box
   (f) They haven't shaded enough boxes (correct answers: A, D, F, H)
   (g) A2

6. Paper 2 Reading questions 2

1 Answer annotated: one source; all the text; key words are 'writer', 'language', 'viewpoints', 'parenting'; 12 minutes
2 (a) Order of bullets in the table: support your ideas with quotations from both texts; compare their different attitudes; compare the methods they use to convey their attitudes
   (b) Answer annotated: two sources; all the texts; key words are 'compare', 'different attitudes', 'children'

7. Skimming for the main idea

1 Answer provided on page 7 of Workbook
2 For example: The opening sentence suggests that the main idea will be the difficulties of teaching, although it also suggests **that the article will be about why teachers find it difficult to control their anger**
3 For example: The end of the article suggests that whilst it is the students who get support, it is the teachers who suffer the most.
4 For example: The ideas expressed at the end of the article differ from those at the beginning as the beginning of the article suggests teachers are aggressive, while the end suggests their careers can be ruined by children's poor behaviour.
5 For example: The main idea in the article is that poor behaviour in schools can make life really difficult for teachers.

8. Annotating the sources

1 Answer provided on page 8 of Workbook
2 Because annotated detail E falls outside the lines of the extract given in the question
3 Answers should include four or five annotations, for example:
   • 'launching a battleship' – suggests war is being declared
   • 'why not the one in our garden?' – suggests the danger is coming closer to home
   • 'There was no warning, either' – gives the impression that people hadn't previously seen them as a threat
   • 'no faintest idea what it was that had hit me' – suggests that the triffids' stings are very powerful and like nothing he has experienced before
   • 'immature' – hints at the idea that a fully grown triffid will be far more dangerous.

9. Putting it into practice

1 (a) and (b) Answers should include four or five annotated words or phrases, for example:
   • 'came under control' – suggests the worst is over
   • 'wind had dropped' – suggests relief, as the threat of the power of the wind is reduced
   • 'towering balloon wavered and tilted and tugged' – gives the idea that the balloon is calmer but still a potential threat

- 'the beast was tamed' – suggests the situation is under control but emphasises the danger the balloon presents in the use of 'beast'
- 'though I did not stop' – 'though' hints at the idea that he may need to pick up his pace again soon.

2 For example: The impression given of the rescue in these lines is that the danger has passed. The reader is told that the situation is 'under control' and that the 'wind had dropped', which suggests relief that the worst is now over. This idea is echoed in the phrase 'the beast was tamed'.

However, these lines also provide hints that this sense of control and relief may only be temporary. For example, the reader learns that the 'towering balloon wavered and tilted and tugged', suggesting that, while it is currently calm, it may rise up again at any moment. This is supported by the metaphor 'beast', which reinforces the idea of the balloon as a wild thing that, in fact, cannot be tamed.

10. Putting it into practice

1 (a) and (b) Answers should include four or five annotated words or phrases, for example:
- 'a pretty loose ship' – suggests lack of rules and discipline
- 'petty prosecutions' – suggests the writer doesn't feel that the majority of children's bad behaviour is worthy of punishment
- 'outer markers' – suggests the writer approaches parenting like a sport
- 'Mothers like a routine' – gives the idea that the writer disagrees with these mothers and takes a different approach
- 'respectable women have found it all very under-regulated' – reinforces the idea that the writer prefers his own approach.

2 For example: Simon Carr has a relaxed attitude to bringing up children. For example, he admits that he runs 'a pretty loose ship', which might imply a lack of rules and discipline. Moreover, the reference to 'petty prosecutions' gives the impression that Carr does not feel that most of his children's bad behaviour deserves to be punished. These ideas are supported by the use of sports terminology such as 'outer markers', which suggests that Carr approaches parenting as if it were a game or sport.

Carr recognises that there are other approaches to parenting and his reference to how 'mothers like a routine' suggests that he disagrees with the idea of a routine and chooses not to follow one. This sense that the writer prefers his own approach is reinforced when he says 'respectable women have found it all very under-regulated'.

11. The writer's viewpoint

Parenting, for example:
- Source 13a – confident attitude displayed towards parenting
- Source 13b – negative and dismissive attitude towards children, revealing a lack of trust

Power of the mind, for example:
- Source 14a – sarcastic tone and hint of fear and suspicion
- Source 14b – sense of awe and admiration of the power of hypnosis

12. Fact, opinion and expert evidence

1 (a) A
  (b) C
  (c) B

2 For example: The writer feels that teaching is made very difficult by poorly behaved children.

3 Fact: 'my… 27-stitch scar'
Opinion: 'supply-teaching hell', '13 is a particularly cruel age'
Expert evidence: 'I passed two 13-year-old girls. "She looks uglier than ever," said they, laughing merrily.'

4 For example:
Fact: The writer includes the fact about the number of stitches to emphasise the cruelty of the girls given the serious nature of her injury.
Opinion: The writer gives her opinion that supply teaching is 'hell' to reinforce the extent of the challenge faced by teachers.
Expert evidence: The writer's own story about the rude 13-year-old girls makes her view that children are poorly behaved seem believable as it comes from an actual experience of behaviour in schools.

13. Explicit information and ideas

Answers could include:
(a) He was halfway out of the basket.
(b) His leg was entangled in the rope.
(c) He was dragged across the field.
(d) He had a boy with him.

14. Implicit information and ideas

1 • The hammer is used to wake them up. – Answer provided on page 14 of Workbook
  • They have to get up at five o'clock. – Explicit
  • The windows are covered with thick frost. – Answer provided on page 14 of Workbook
  • The sun is not yet up. – Implicit

2 Answers should include four implicit ideas, for example:
(a) Conditions are over-crowded.
(b) There is no adequate bedding to keep them warm.
(c) They have no proper toilet facilities.
(d) Their boots are usually worn wet.

15. Inference

1 Annotations could include:
- 'I didn't look any more than I had to.'
- 'Mrs Dubose would catch him'
- 'anywhere to keep from looking at her'

2 For example:
(a) The extract suggests that Mrs Dubose is **frightening, as the sentence, 'I didn't look any more than I had to' gives the impression that the narrator is scared of her.**
(b) The phrase 'Mrs Dubose would catch him' creates the idea that Mrs Dubose is fierce and someone to be wary of.

3 For example:
Mrs Dubose's house seems intimidating from the start of the extract, as it has 'steep front steps'. The house also frightens the children as they are met by an 'oppressive odour', which makes the narrator 'afraid, expectant' and 'watchful'. The odour is described as something usually smelt in 'rain-rotted' houses, which gives the reader the impression that the house **is old, uncared for and possibly unsafe. There is also a suggestion that the house is unclean when the writer uses the description 'unbleached domestic sheets'. It seems**

clear that the house is not a pleasant place to be as the reader is told that the narrator feels 'afraid, expectant, watchful'.

This sense of intimidation and fear continues with the introduction of Mrs Dubose. She initially seems vulnerable as she is described as 'lying under a pile of quilts', and the descriptions of the 'glass with a teaspoon' and the 'ear syringe' suggest she may be unwell. However, the phrases 'for a moment' and 'almost friendly' indicate that Mrs Dubose may not be welcoming and this is reinforced in her first, hostile words, when she describes the narrator as 'dirty'.

16. Point–Evidence–Explain

1 Evidence B

2 Evidence B is the most effective because it is an example of a list of adjectives and therefore links directly to the point made.

3 Evidence: For example, she uses the words [for example] 'barricaded', 'trapping' and 'threatened'. Explanation B

4 For example: Explanation B is more effective because it is fully developed and more specific, suggesting that the teacher treated the children like prisoners. The word 'also' signals additional details, which explore the teacher's actions further.

17. Putting it into practice

1 For example:
   (a) They grew quietly without drawing attention to themselves.
   (b) Nobody took any notice of them.
   (c) Scientific experts were excited about them.
   (d) The public had no knowledge about the triffids.

2 Answers could include these key points:
- the triffids attracted a lot of press attention and news people 'were quickly off the mark', which suggests they were initially viewed as a new type of sport
- news people fly to 'outlandish places', which suggests excitement
- 'sandwiched between a hula contest' and jokes such as 'educate our potatoes' give the impression they are not taken seriously
- hyperbole and alliteration are used in the news announcement 'Vegetables on vacation!', suggesting the triffids are viewed as comical and harmless
- 'hangover' indicates there is a party atmosphere in response to the triffids
- the narrator is 'fascinated'
- the exclamation mark after 'walking' suggests ordinary people are becoming excited.

18. Putting it into practice

Answers could include these key points:
- personal, direct style appeals to the reader – 'you can make the subject think …'
- use of powerful verbs to generate interest and make hypnotism sound exciting, innovative and dangerous – 'transformed, dazed, abolished, obliterated'
- similes used to add humour and reflect the sense of awe – 'ammonia will smell to him like cologne water'
- hyperbole used to create particular effects – 'legs and breasts may be amputated'.

19. Word classes

1 • Noun – for example, 'furniture', 'handbag'
   • Verb – Answer provided on page 19 of Workbook
   • Adverb – Answer provided on page 19 of Workbook
   • Adjective – for example, 'insolent', 'noisy'

2 For example: The lists of adjectives build up contrasting pictures in a reader's mind of what teenagers are like. For instance, 'polite, quiet and co-operative' creates a positive image, whilst 'insolent, noisy, crabby…' creates a negative image. This will make the reader question their own view of teenagers.

3 For example:
   (a) The action verb 'dig' suggests very hard physical labour, which reinforces the hardships of the labour camp in the mind of the reader.
   (b) The verb 'run' is effective because it reminds the reader that the prisoners are unable to run away and that there is no escape.

20. Connotations

1 (a) outer markers – border, sport
       perimeter – extreme edge, limits, outskirts
       boundaries – cricket pitch, limits, dividing line
   (b) For example: While the words 'outer markers', 'perimeter' and 'boundaries' suggest that the writer sees parenting as a sport, they also indicate that he does give his children limits and that they have to pay attention to these limits.

2 For example:
   (a) The adjective 'rain-rotted' has connotations of neglect and decay, and suggests that Mrs Dubose's house might also be old, crumbling and worn.
   (b) The 'coal-oil lamps' have old-fashioned connotations and give the impression of a dark, smoky space.

21. Figurative language

1 For example:
   The writer uses the simile 'like a glacier', which has connotations of **icy cold, arctic conditions and something that is hard, sharp and dangerous.** This suggests to the reader **that Mrs Dubose is cold, harsh and unfriendly.**

2 For example:
   The simile 'like a clam hole at low tide' suggests a wide, dirty opening. This gives the reader an impression of Mrs Dubose that is foul and unattractive.
   The suggestion in the simile 'like some viscous substance coming to a boil' is that Mrs Dubose is capable of hurting others with what she says.

3 Mrs Dubose is presented as repulsive and frightening in appearance. For example, the metaphor 'cords of saliva' suggests that thick strands of saliva cover her mouth. This presents her to the reader as unhuman and creates a frightening vision of her mouth as something dangerous.

22. Creation of character

1 The writer uses dialogue to show that Mrs Dubose is rude as she calls Jem's sister 'dirty'. However, Jem's dialogue shows that he is **brave and 'quietly' able to stand up to Mrs Dubose, even if his defiant words 'I ain't scared of you' suggest that he may be a little more afraid than he is letting on. His words also show that he is protective of his sister when he contradicts Mrs Dubose, saying that she 'ain't dirty'.**

2 Answers could include these key points:
- 're-opened' suggests that Jem is not intimidated by Mrs Dubose
- 'read too fast' and 'skipped' suggest he is reckless as he is trying to fool Mrs Dubose
- 'dangling in mid-air' suggests he is brave.

3 Answers could include these key points:
- Description – a very detailed, unattractive image of Mrs Dubose is built up through:
  - figurative language – such as 'like a glacier', 'cords of saliva', 'like a clam hole at low tide', 'like some viscous substance coming to a boil'
  - carefully chosen adjectives – such as 'horrible', 'dirty', 'pinpoint', 'knobby'
- Action – Mrs Dubose's actions suggest she is, for example:
  - physically unattractive – 'she would draw her nether lip to her upper plate and carry her chin with it'
  - harsh and a little cruel – 'catch him and make him'.

23. Creating atmosphere

1 For example:
'rage' – uncontrollable force, suggests the wind is violent
'force'– suggests strength and violence
'struck' – hurt, damage, suggests the wind is a weapon

2 For example:
Action verbs – 'struck', 'broke', 'flew', 'rose'
Personification (of the balloon) – 'innocent comical wagging'
Adjectives – 'innocent', 'comical', 'ridged'

3 (a) Answer extract B
(b) For example: Answer extract B is the most effective as it uses a clear P-E-E structure and fully explains the connotations of 'rage' and 'force'.

4 For example: Overall, the writer creates an atmosphere of **tension and danger by personifying the wind and describing in detail the actions of the rescuers.**

24. Narrative voice

1 Extract A: (a)
Extract B: (c)
Extract C: (b)

2 Answers could include these key points about the first person narration:
- shows how scornful he is of others – 'Incompetence came off him like heat'
- shows his complete confidence in his own ability – 'the tragedy would not have happened'.

25. Putting it into practice

Answers could include these key points:
- overall – build-up of action using strong verbs, together with vivid picture of the balloon creates drama and tension
- description of the balloon emphasises scale of problem – 'the size of a house'
- imagery for the balloon – 'the shape of a teardrop'
- personification of the balloon, and use of strong and action verbs, emphasises the scale of the problem – 'gusted', 'pushed' and 'lifted'
- verbs used for the rescuers' actions suggest desperation and a battle with the balloon – 'clutching', 'bumping', 'trying', 'lunging', 'snatched' (which also has connotations of stealing, running away with)
- verbs used to highlight the power of the wind and the balloon – 'tossed from one side to another' makes the boy seem helpless, like a rag doll.

26. Putting it into practice

Answers could include these key points:
- use of facts – '25,000 teachers needed', '£58–75 salary compared to a poor governess', 'hours of work'
- describes the government certificate as 'much sought after'
- positive adjectives used to describe the life of a teacher – 'healthful', ' congenial', 'eminently tempting'.

27. Rhetorical devices 1

1 For example, four of:
- pattern of three – 'polite, quiet and cooperative'
- lists – 'insolent, noisy, crabby, offensive, …'
- alliteration – 'skulking, smoking'
- rhetorical questions – 'But why shocking?'
- colloquial language –'lost it', 'whingeing', 'shut the little toads up'.

2 For example (taking the example of colloquial language): … The writer also uses **colloquial language at the start of the article when she states that the teacher 'lost it' in class. The writer uses this conversational tone to suggest that the teacher behaved like a teenager. As this phrase is used by young people to describe losing control, it will encourage readers to make a negative judgement about the teacher.**

28. Rhetorical devices 2

1 For example: The repetition of 'Mothers' at the start of two sentences is a little sarcastic as it seems to mock their importance. The writer then repeats the word 'routine' to emphasise the way mothers rely on rules. This makes routines sound petty, particularly as it is followed by humorous comments that show the writer has no routine whatsoever in his house.

2 For example: The words 'no particular order' suggest there is no routine in the writer's household, that all rules are equal and they can be applied at any time. This contrasts with the bedtime routine preferred by mothers, where there is a clear structure, which in turn emphasises the writer's relaxed attitude to parenting.

3 For example: Hyperbole: The phrase 'Except damn, of course, and hell' is used to add humour as it exaggerates the unusual rules the writer has put in place.
Emotive language: The emotive language in 'Screaming insanely' is used to build a picture for the reader of a fun and relaxed household.

29. Whole text structure: fiction

1 For example:
The underlined sentences show that the balloon is already out of control and that the pilot is in difficulty. This suggests to the reader that the danger ahead will be far greater as they will not be able to rely on the pilot for experienced help.

2 For example:
The writer withholds the fact that there is a boy in the basket as this structure increases the tension for the reader. Before this fact is revealed, the writer closely describes **the balloon, using the similes 'the size of a house' and 'the shape of a teardrop' to give the reader an idea of the scale of the crisis. The personification of the wind in 'pushed and lifted' also builds tension by highlighting its power.**

The revelation that there is a boy in the basket increases the tension because **readers already know the pilot is tangled up in the rope and that the balloon is out of control. The tension is also increased by the mention of the boy's young age in the final part of the sentence.**

3 Answers should include comments about the writer's use of closely described detail and action, which emphasise the length of time the rescue takes and how difficult it is.

30. Whole text structure: non-fiction

1 For example: Hanson starts her article by shocking readers with a vivid and detailed description of a teacher who 'lost it' in class. Readers will want to read on to find out the rest of the story, and to find out how Hanson really feels about teachers.

2 Warnings – Hanson wants readers to think carefully about behaviour in the classroom, and the effects this could have on teachers' careers.

3 For example:
Initially, Arlidge is scared about the idea of having two electrodes attached to his head. This is implied in the phrase 'pumping electricity straight into my brain'. However, when he actually tries the electrodes, his tone changes. **This is signalled in the short sentence 'And then something remarkable happens', which draws attention to a shift in his reaction to what is happening. This is then followed by two longer sentences creating a positive picture of 'waves gently flowing', which reflect his calmer state of mind. The verb 'slump' contrasts with the earlier verb 'pumping' and suggests a complete change in mood.**

31. Identifying sentence types

1 Sentence A is a single-clause sentence.
Sentence C is a multi-clause sentence (coordinate).
Sentence B is a multi-clause sentence (subordinate).
Sentence D is a minor sentence.

2 For example:
Single-clause: 'Now think of that young teacher.'
Multi-clause (subordinate): 'The end of her torment was a whisker away, but, driven barmy by pupils, she still blew it.'
Multi-clause (coordinate): 'She had probably been shouted at and humiliated for 40 minutes.'
Minor: 'The pathetic little wets.'

32. Commenting on sentences

1 For example: The series of quicker, short sentences at the beginning of the extract suggests an initial atmosphere of tension and fear. The longer sentence slows the extract down and reflects the new sense of calm in the scene being described.

2 For example:
The writer starts the paragraph with a short, single-clause sentence **and the next few sentences are similarly short. These are used to present the basic facts of the scene and leave the reader wanting more details.**
After using short sentences, the writer then uses a multi-clause sentence. This adds to the tension **because the structure of the sentence builds up the sense of danger and keeps the reader waiting for the climax of the rescue.**
The writer then uses two multi-clause sentences that end with subordinate clauses. This adds to the tension **as the first multi-clause sentence suggests bravery, while the second increases the sense of anticipation by delaying the most worrying information until the final clause.**

33. Putting it into practice

Answers could include these key points:
- starts on a positive note – 'incite an investigating spirit'
- sounds exciting – 'trick like that'
- use of ellipsis at ends of paragraphs creates cliff-hangers
- short paragraph ('About ten minutes after…') continues the excited tone, then 'Unfortunately' at the beginning of the next paragraph suggests a change in tone
- closely described detail of the narrator's actions draws out the sense of tension.

34. Putting it into practice

Answers could include these key points.
Language:
- use of facts (for example, 'Mankind has used mood-altering substances ever since we discovered alcohol…') make the article more believable and opinions (for example, 'the most off-the-chart business brains') show that the writer feels that these people should be admired
- use of expert evidence throughout (for example, 'Goldwasser assures me') makes the writer sound reliable, as does the later information about the experts' backgrounds and qualifications
- hyperbole ('pumping electricity' and 'hack my brain') exaggerates the writer's fear for comic effect
- lists ('willpower, self-control, motivation, confidence and creativity') suggest the mind-altering technique could have many helpful uses
- repetition ('tap into') makes technique sound very positive and enjoyable.

Structure:
- starts by hinting at the writer's fear ('Try to relax'), to make readers want to find out what exactly has frightened him
- change in tone ('And then something remarkable happens') entertains as it shows surprise that the technique works
- variety of sentence structures is used to suggest the writer is nervous when the electricity is turned on.

35. Evaluating a fiction text 1

1 All options should be circled except: 'Focus closely on individual words and phrases, explaining connotations in detail.' This should not be circled as it is only necessary to write about the **overall impression** created by a word/phrase, rather than writing in depth about language techniques and the connotations of individual words.

2 (a) 'We were all talking at once' – Answer provided on page 35 of Workbook
'myself and the motorist' links to 'he then puts himself first when explaining an idea'
'Someone … Someone' links to 'The writer uses repetition'

(b) For example: The narrator does not appear to be a natural leader at the start of this section as he **admits he is the same as the other men when he says 'we were all talking at once'.**
However, he then puts himself first when explaining an idea, for example **in the phrase 'myself and the motorist'. This gives the impression that he feels his input is the most important.**
The writer uses repetition to **reinforce this idea that the narrator is the natural leader in the scene. The repeated word 'Someone' suggests that no one else stands out, as the other men are not given names.**

3 The evidence selected should recognise that the narrator is **not** shown to be a natural leader throughout the extract. For example: 'I must have been a hundred yards away when the situation came under control.'

36. Evaluating a fiction text 2
Other examples could include:
- References to Mrs Dubose's illness encourages the reader to sympathise with her predicament.
- The harsh description of her appearance presents her as threatening, therefore reducing our sympathy.

37. Using evidence to evaluate
1 Answers could include references to the narrator's:
- inquisitive nature, which should be admired
- reckless attitude in confronting the dangerous plant
- ignorance to the danger he was in
- bravery for attempting to explore and gain new knowledge.

2 (b) Include it as part of your sentence. (All other statements are things you should do when using longer quotations.)

38. Putting it into practice
Answers could include these key points:
- Shukhov does not get up straight away
- he has found a way to keep warm and ignore others – 'head buried in a blanket and a coat'
- he understands what happens in the camp – 'his ears told him everything going on', and list of what is happening outside his room
- he understands how hard the work is – 'dig pits and put up posts'
- despite the hard work to come, he knows how to cope – 'warm up with the work'
- he understands who to bribe to make life easier – 'take a pound of pork fat to the senior official'
- the extract ends on this note – he knows how to get out of the work, 'get a few days off'
- whole extract – most of the extract suggests he knows how the camp works and has come to terms with it.

39. Writing about two texts
1 separate
2 Assessment objective 3
3 (a) Paper 2
   (b) Question 4
   (c) Question 2
   (d) Question 2
   (e) Question 4
   (f) Question 4

40. Selecting evidence for synthesis
1 Use details from **both** sources. Write a summary of the positive aspects of mind-altering techniques.
2 (a) (i); (b) (i)
3 For example, from *The Boys Are Back in Town*:
- mothers 'take a more active interest in the details'
- 'Mothers like a routine'
- 'The bath before bedtime calms them down'.
For example, from 'The Rearing and Management of Children':
- 'simply in not doing as the babe demands'
- 'Obedience is the first lesson to be taught'
- 'With respect to the time of feeding, irregularity should be guarded against'.

41. Answering a synthesis question
1 Similarly, likewise, both, in the same way, also
2 For example: You should use adverbials in your synthesis to link together the similarities you find between the two texts.
3 (a) Overview C
   (b) For example: Overview C shows an understanding of the specific similarity between the two texts.
4 Answers should use suitable adverbials and start with the overview identified in Question 3 (a) above. For example: Both writers feel that mind-altering techniques can have a positive impact on health and happiness. For instance, Arlidge quotes an expert who feels that mind-altering techniques can have an impact on the treatment of 'obesity, alcoholism' and 'gambling addiction'. 'Victorian Hypnotism' also stresses the health benefits of mind-altering as the writer feels that hypnotism can allow 'the most painful experiences' to be endured without any anaesthetic.

42. Looking closely at language
1 'bonkers' – Answer provided on page 42 of Workbook
'gizmos' – means 'modern gadgets', an informal term with trendy connotations
'wearable kit' – suggests fashionable and essential, rather than functional, items
2 For example: The colloquial language of 'bonkers', meaning 'mad' or 'crazy', creates an informal tone with positive connotations. The word 'gizmos' and the phrase 'wearable kit' both suggest fashionable items rather than functional ones, which creates the impression that the writer does not really take the new technology seriously.
3 For example: The three subordinate clauses contain more factual information about the purpose of the devices, such as 'monitoring our blood pressure'. This gives the sentence a more serious and scientific tone.
4 (a) For example: The repetition of 'tap into' makes changing the way we feel sound simple.
   (b) For example: The long sentence that follows the repetition in the four short sentences creates a reassuring effect, which persuades the reader that this is something they might want to try.

43. Planning to compare language
1 Completed plans should include example quotations and explanations.
For example, for Extract 1:
Tone – formal language, for example 'The duties of teachers', 'The hours of work' – suggests order and authority
Rhetorical devices/language – formal language, for example 'free for recreation' – gives a positive image of life for teachers
Sentences – longer sentences with subordinate clauses deliver a lot of detail, which adds to the authoritative tone

44. Comparing language
1 For example:
   (a) Short sentences for dramatic effect.
   (b) Lists to reinforce rules.
2 For example:
   (a) To explain that children need to be controlled.
   (b) Extract 1: Facts and sophisticated language
      Extract 2: Humour and informal language

45. Comparing structure

Answers could include these key points:
- Cassell ends the article by commenting on the appeal of teaching, therefore linking back to the opening section about recruitment. The ending also reinforces the derogatory attitude towards women that has been evident throughout the article.
- Hanson ends with a link to the beginning, focusing on the teacher who couldn't cope with the stress of poor behaviour. The tone is comical and light-hearted though still supportive of the challenges teachers face.

46. Comparing ideas

1 (a) Both texts start by expressing ideas about **problems in the education system.**
    (b) Hanson feels **that the main problem is the behaviour of students in the classroom** whereas 'Occupations Accessible to Women' **suggests that the biggest difficulty is the lack of suitably qualified teachers.**
2 Text 1: Supply teaching is very challenging – 'supply-teaching hell'
    Text 2: Teaching is a rewarding and pleasant profession – 'The duties of teachers in elementary schools are both healthful and congenial'
3 For example: Both texts focus on the nature of teaching and its effect on teachers. Hanson uses hyperbole to argue that supply teaching is very challenging as she calls it 'supply-teaching hell'. On the other hand, the view in 'Occupations Accessible to Women' is expressed in more formal language. Teaching is called 'both healthful and congenial', suggesting that it is a rewarding and pleasant profession.

47. Comparing perspective

1 For example: The writer of 'The Rearing and Management of Children' believes children need firm rules, whereas Simon Carr's perspective on parenting appears to be far less rigid.
2 For example: In 'The Rearing and Management of Children', the writer uses the emotive phrase 'a serious delusion', which helps to show the writer's strong feelings about obedience. In *The Boys Are Back in Town*, **Carr uses more informal and colloquial phrases, such as 'pretty loose ship' and 'fuzzy logic', to show that he is more relaxed about the behaviour of his children.**
3 Answers should consist of two P-E-E paragraphs. The paragraphs should use one piece of evidence from each of the extracts and suitable adverbials. Answers could include these key points:
    - both texts maintain the same perspective throughout
    - Carr ends with a colloquial term 'semi-feral'
    - 'The Rearing and Management of Children' ends with the formal phrase 'implanting a spirit of obedience'.

48. Answering a comparison question

Answers should:
- compare the language in the two texts
- focus on the effect of the writer's language choices
- support key points with evidence and explanation/analysis.

49. Putting it into practice

Answers could include these key points:
The Boys are Back in Town:
- the writer has a relaxed attitude to parenting and believes children should not be too restricted by rules
- colloquial language – 'pretty loose ship', 'fuzzy logic'

- words that suggest sport – 'outer marker', 'boundaries', 'perimeter'
- one sentence paragraph – 'Fewer rules…'
- repetition of 'mothers' and 'routine'
- paragraph of lists using short sentences – 'No interrupting adults'
- words/phrases with animal connotations – 'Free-range', 'feral'.

'The Rearing and Management of Children':
- the writer feels that children should be given clear rules and boundaries
- repetition – 'No harsh words, no impatient gestures'
- formal language – 'habits of obedience'
- words/phrases with connotations of strictness and discipline – 'enforce the rules', 'requires great firmness in checking'
- detailed examples to back up points – 'Taking food as an example…'
- emotive language – 'depraved', 'exposed', 'rejected'.

Section B: Writing

50. Writing questions: an overview

1 (a) Paper 1
    (b) Paper 2
    (c) Paper 1   Paper 2
    (d) Paper 2
    (e) Paper 2
2 (a) Assessment objective 5
    (b) Both
    (c) Assessment objective 6
    (d) Assessment objective 6
    (e) Assessment objective 5
    (f) Assessment objective 5
3 For example:
    Assessment objective 5 (a) – Write fluently and engagingly using appropriate techniques to suit a variety of audiences, purposes and styles.
    Assessment objective 5 (b) – Arrange ideas effectively using appropriate techniques to ensure the text is clear.
    Assessment objective 6 – Use a wide selection of words in a range of sentence styles, and accurate spelling and punctuation throughout.

51. Writing questions: Paper 1

1 (a) True
    (b) False
    (c) False
    (d) True
2 (a) story
    (b) For example: An account of a person, object or event.
3

Form	Description or narrative
Purpose	To be imaginative and engaging
Audience	Suitable for adults

52. Writing questions: Paper 2

1 argue, inform, persuade, explain
2 (a) local newspaper (readers)
    (b) article
    (c) explain point of view
3 For example:
    - Teenagers may be out at clubs and activities and not be able to get back home for 9 pm.

- Police would need to enforce this, taking up valuable police time.
- Parents would need to be at home checking that their children were home at 9 pm.

53. Writing questions: time management

1

Total time for Paper 1, Section B: Writing	45 minutes
Planning your answer	5 minutes
Writing your answer	35 minutes
Checking and proofreading your answer	5 minutes
Total time for Paper 2, Section B: Writing	45 minutes
Planning your answer	5 minutes
Writing your answer	35 minutes
Checking and proofreading your answer	5 minutes

2 (a) False
  (b) True
  (c) False
  (d) True
  (e) False
  (f) False
3 (a) Answer provided on page 53 of Workbook
  (b) Will my target reader be engaged by this?
  (c) Am I achieving my purpose?
  (d) Am I making a range of points or repeating myself?
  (e) Should I be moving on to my next point now?
  (f) How much time have I got left?

54. Writing for a purpose: creative 1

1 For example:
see: a kaleidoscope of brilliant colours
hear: screeching crowds on the rollercoasters
smell: Answer provided on page 54 of Workbook
touch: the excited grip of my sister's warm hand
taste: Answer provided on page 54 of Workbook
2 For example: My face lit up with a wide smile and **my excitement mounted as I pushed through the crowds and stole my first glimpse of the brightly lit rides.**
3 For example:
Simile: colours as bright and dazzling as a firework display
Metaphor: rides towering over us
Personification: the darkness swallowed us as our ride on the ghost train began
4 Answers should:
- use the senses
- include examples of figurative language
- include examples of carefully chosen language
- use verbs that show rather than tell
- maintain one narrative voice throughout.
For example: My face lit up with a wide smile and my excitement mounted as I pushed through the crowds and stole my first glimpse of the brightly lit rides. A kaleidoscope of colours as bright and dazzling as a firework display met my eager eyes and, inhaling deeply, I could almost taste the syrupy sweet candy-floss on sale nearby. I squeezed my sister's hand and grinned.

55. Writing for a purpose: creative 2

1 (a) Narrative voice – first person
  (b) Engaging the reader – for example: senses ('I shivered'), feelings ('I was looking forward to the trip'), figurative language ('like a gun being fired')
  (c) Structure – for example: hints at what's to come ('seemed cross')
2 For example:
Show rather than tell – for example, describe the autumn scene rather than saying 'It was November'; show how the narrator's body language and actions suggest feelings of pleasure and excitement instead of stating 'I was looking forward to the trip'.
Use a range of senses to help the reader experience the scene.
Choose language carefully and for effect, using powerful adjectives, verbs and adverbs.
Make figurative language as powerful as possible to draw the reader into the scene.
Engage the reader from the start with a strong opening that doesn't reveal all the answers and encourages the reader to wonder where the narrator is going and what will happen next.
3 For example:
I leaned over to the window and glanced up at the station clock, a broad smile on my lips. I shivered. Hugging the quilt of my parka close, I noticed the trail of limp leaves on the carriage floor, as though the season, with its warming display of reds, yellows and oranges, had decided to come along for the ride.
The train jolted into life and was soon winding through the suburbs, picking up speed. Once out of the grey and the concrete, it shot through isolated, rural stations like a bullet, aiming straight for the next sprawling metropolis.
The woman opposite looked up at me from her knitting. Her brow was furrowed, her mouth small and tight. She was furious.

56. Writing for a purpose: viewpoint 1

1 Examples of points **for** the suggestion could include: people spend hours on the internet; like other addictive drugs, people's use increases the more they use it, meaning they become more and more dependent; people denied access can suffer cravings.
Examples of points **against** the suggestion could include: the time people spend on the internet shows how useful it is; it does not cause physical harm; using the internet is no different to reading a book or meeting friends, except it is onscreen.
2 Answers will vary. Remember that you can make evidence up, as long as it is believable. For example:
For the suggestion: point – people spend hours on the internet; evidence – 75% of all teenagers admit to spending at least two hours online every day.
Against the suggestion: point – using the internet is no different to reading a book or meeting friends, except it is onscreen; evidence – research conducted by Professor Nett and his team show that people who interact online rather than face-to-face have an equally healthy social life.
3 For example:
For – Some people might feel **that we spend too much time on the internet.** However, **it is clear from the number of hours that people spend online on a daily basis that the internet is an invaluable resource in the modern age.**
Against – Some people might feel **that the internet is not a danger as it does not cause physical harm.**

However, **recent studies clearly show a rise in back, neck and wrist injuries resulting from extended periods in front of the screen and over-use of the mouse.**

4 For example: lists: Some people might feel **that the internet is not a danger as it does not cause physical harm.** However, **recent studies clearly show a rise in the numbers of internet users suffering from back pain, repetitive strain injury in the wrist and forearm, blurred vision and poor concentration.**

57. Writing for a purpose: viewpoint 2

1 (a) Answer provided on page 57 of Workbook
   For example:
   (b) New services for teenagers
   (c) Teenager-friendly opening times
   (d) Providing a study zone for teenagers

2 Remember that you can make facts and statistics up, as long as they are believable. For example:
   (a) More than 50% of teenagers have not considered using the local library for study.
   (b) Over three-quarters of teenagers said they might use the local library if facilities were improved.
   (c) Extending opening times to 7pm would attract students after school hours.
   (d) 95% of all teenagers said they would be more likely to use the library if there was a special study zone.

3 Answers might include subheadings and should include examples of facts and statistics. The tone of the writing should be formal. For example:
   The local library currently works hard to offer a broad and flexible service. Nonetheless, more than half of local teenagers have not considered using the facilities for study purposes. This suggests that, while the library's efforts to attract the attention of other sections of society have been successful, it is currently failing to appeal to those aged 18 and under.

58. Writing for an audience

1 For example: The audience is likely to be **adults of both genders, probably those aged over 25, although younger people may read the article as it concerns them.**

2 Sentence B – The tone and vocabulary in this sentence are formal, which is appropriate for a national newspaper article whose audience is mainly adults.

3 Answers should be appropriate for a teenage audience, and may include some informal language although non-standard English, including slang and texting language, should be avoided. A variety of sentence structures and a wide vocabulary should also be used. For example:
   To begin with, while green, leafy vegetables may not appeal to your taste buds, they are nonetheless packed with fibre, vitamins and minerals. Their health benefits are widely acknowledged: apart from great skin and bundles of energy, these greens are thought to help protect you from diseases like diabetes, and possibly even cancer.

59. Putting it into practice

1 (a) Student's choice of question option.
   (b) Planning time: 10 minutes
       Writing time: 30 minutes
       Checking time: 5 minutes
   (c) Description – audience: teachers; purpose: to describe image; image: photo of coral reef
       Narrative – audience: teachers; purpose: to write a story; voice: first or third person

2 Examples of descriptive techniques should be suitable for the title chosen in part 1 (a). Techniques used might include: using the senses, figurative language, language choice, etc.

60. Putting it into practice

1

Timing	Plan: 5 minutes Write: 35 minutes Check: 5 minutes
Topic	Dogs banned from parks
Form	Newspaper article
Audience	Probably adults of both genders
Purpose	To argue/persuade
Key features	Key points, evidence, counter-arguments, adverbials, rhetorical devices

61. Form: articles

1–5 Answers will vary but should include a headline, subheading, an opening paragraph summing up their ideas and a concluding paragraph. They may also include a quotation.

62. Form: letters and reports

1 (a) True
   (b) True
   (c) False (you should use 'Yours faithfully' if you have used 'Dear Sir/Madam')
   (d) True

2 For example:
   Heading: Youth Parliaments
   Opening sentence: Many councils across the UK and Europe have set up youth parliaments and have found them to be an effective way to access the views of young people.

3 Answers should suggest two recommendations, which could include:
   (a) setting up a Facebook page
   (b) visiting schools and colleges.

63. Form: speeches

(a) F, (b) D, (c) A, (d) G, (e) B, (f) C, (g) E, (h) H
Answers will vary but should include some of the techniques mentioned in Question 1.

64. Putting it into practice

1 Answers should be suitable for an adult audience and should include:
   • a title
   • an introduction
   • details of the current situation and some appropriate recommendations
   • facts/statistics to support the recommendations
   • a conclusion.

65. Ideas and planning: creative

1 Answers will vary but should include either a spider diagram or a list describing the scene.

2 Details added to the plan could include dialogue, personification and other figurative devices.

66. Structure: creative

1 Answers will vary but all should:
- complete the narrative structure with a balanced amount of detail for each stage
- include ideas about creative writing techniques.

For example:

Exposition: Relaxing in front of fire on windy winter day. Doorbell rings. I answer – it is my long-lost sister. Use dialogue to introduce her character.

Complication: In kitchen, making tea – use senses. Sister starts to tell me where she's been all these years. Depict sister – show not tell, simile/metaphor to describe her manner.

Crisis: Reveals she's been living in Peru, where she set up an organisation to help the poor; personification to express my surprise.

Resolution: She invites me to go out there for the summer to help with her work; action verbs.

2 As for Question 1. Answers should adapt the answer to Question 1 and follow the flashback structure given in the Workbook. For example:

Crisis: Reveals she's been living in Peru, where she set up an organisation to help the poor; personification to express my surprise.

Exposition: Relaxing in front of fire on windy winter day. Doorbell rings. I answer – it is my long-lost sister. Use dialogue to introduce her character.

Complication: In kitchen, making tea – use senses. Sister starts to tell me where she's been all these years. Depict sister – show not tell, simile/metaphor to describe her manner.

Return to crisis: Sister telling me about Peru.

Resolution: She invites me to go out there for the summer to help with her work; action verbs.

67. Beginnings and endings: creative

1 Beginnings should not over-use dialogue and should contain appropriate figurative devices and language techniques. For example, for 'Conflict or danger':
The envelope burned in my hand. To open it was, I knew, to enter a different world where I would never be completely safe again. My heart thundered in my chest and my blood boiled past my ears.

2 Answers will vary depending on the opening chosen from Question 1.

3 Answers should reflect the tone decided on in Question 2.

68. Putting it into practice

1 Plans for the narrative should include:
- some form of four-part narrative structure – either a flow diagram or a spider diagram
- ideas for beginning or ending
- details of narrative voice and creative writing techniques to be used.

69. Ideas and planning: viewpoint 1

1 Plans should include:
- an introduction and a conclusion
- three sequenced key points
- supporting evidence
- a counter-argument.

70. Ideas and planning: viewpoint 2

1 Plans should include:
- an introduction and a conclusion
- three or four sequenced key points
- a range of supporting ideas and details.

71. Openings: viewpoint

1 For example:
Rhetorical question – Is prison the answer to serious crime?
Bold or controversial statement – Prison has never been less effective in preventing serious crime.
Relevant quotation – 'Prison saved me. It turned my life around.'
Shocking or surprising fact or statistic – No less than 58% of offenders sentenced to less than a year in prison go on to reoffend.
Short, relevant, interesting anecdote – Answer provided on page 71 of Workbook

2 Answers will vary but all should:
- make clear the topic/argument
- include one or two of the suggested approaches from Question 1.

72. Conclusions: viewpoint

1 For example:
Vivid image – As the colossal prison door swings shut behind yet another serial offender, so too does the window of opportunity to make a real change.
Warning – If alternatives to prison sentences are not found soon, serious crime rates will only continue to rise.
Happy note – Crime may not pay, but with serious crime rates on the decrease, sending offenders to prison certainly does.
Thought-provoking question – Answer provided on page 72 of Workbook
'Call to action' – We must call on the government to think again about their approach to prison sentences. Now is the time for change.
Refer to introduction – So, prison is not the whole answer to serious crime, but it is a vital part of the solution.

2 Answers will vary but all should include one or two of the suggested approaches from Question 1.

73. Putting it into practice

1 Plans should include:
- an engaging title
- subheadings
- an idea for an engaging opening paragraph
- ideas for about three sequenced paragraphs, with details of figurative language to be used
- an idea for the conclusion.

74. Paragraphing

1 Point: 'When students choose their GCSE options' to 'help them in their future career'.
Evidence: 'I chose my GCSEs' to 'because lots of my friends had chosen that subject'.
Explain: 'Neither of these reasons are sound' to 'more informed and more sensible decisions'.

2 For example:
Point: The careers advice currently available to students is inadequate.
Evidence: Students make poor choices about which subjects to continue to study.
Explain: Students find themselves ill-prepared or unable to pursue the career that best suits them.

3 While schools and colleges do offer some careers advice to students, the advice is frequently inadequate, failing to outline clearly all possible career paths students may wish to follow. This is clear in the poor choices students make about which subjects to continue studying, which often do not support their ideal career. As a result, students find themselves ill-prepared or unable to

pursue the career they are best suited to, a situation which could be prevented with more and improved careers advice.

4 Point: 'While schools and colleges' to 'may wish to follow'.
Evidence: 'This is clear' to 'their ideal career'.
Explain: 'As a result' to 'improved careers advice'.

75. Linking ideas

1

Adding an idea	Explaining	Illustrating
Furthermore…	Consequently	For example
Moreover…	Therefore	For instance

Emphasising	Comparing	Contrasting
In particular	In the same way	However
Significantly	Similarly	On the other hand

2 Extract 1 examples: For example…; therefore…
Extract 2 examples: Moreover… ; Significantly…; for instance…

3 Answers will vary but all should use a P-E-E structure and feature a range of adverbials. For example: Exams cannot give a fair and accurate picture of a student's real abilities as too much is dependent on the day of the exam and how the student is feeling on that particular day. For instance, a student might be highly competent and have worked hard to prepare for the exam. However, they may also have had a sleepless night or be struggling with an illness on the day of the exam, which may lead to poorer marks than they might otherwise have attained. Consequently, exams are not only an unrepresentative but also an unfair means of assessing a student's ability.

76. Putting it into practice

1 Answers should be suitable for an adult audience and should include:
• a title
• an introduction
• details of the current situation and some appropriate recommendations
• facts/statistics to support the recommendations
• a conclusion.

77. Formality and standard English 1

1 **Standard English** is the very formal aspect of English that is held by many to be the 'correct' or 'accepted' way of communicating that is not influenced or affected by different variations in regional dialect.
Slang is language at its most informal, which can be described as non-standard and ungrammatical. It is often used within small social groups and can be considered offensive in some cases.
Colloquial language is informal language that is not rude, but would not be used in formal situations and is often used in speech.
Register is the variety of language used for a particular purpose or in a particular social setting.

2 (a) Advice could include:
• be more formal in the way you address your audience – Dear Sir/Madam (or their surname)
• don't be confrontational
• avoid using slang
• make sure that you use correct punctuation.
(b) Answers will vary but should follow the advice given above.

3 Advice could include: Start with an informal sentence to draw in your audience, for example: Have you had enough of revision? Do you want some easy tips on how to manage your time so you can chill out more? Please read our handy guide that could make life far easier for yourself (and probably your friends and family who you are driving nuts by now!)

78. Formality and standard English 2

1 Many people think … Both
I think computer games … Both
It could be argued … A
It's only oldies … B
What is wrong … Both
There ain't nothing like … B

2 For example: Video gaming is a well-established and popular activity for many teenagers. Whilst the older generation might have spent their teenage years watching television and chatting on the phone, we communicate and interact with our friends through online games. It is all part of the way we interact with each other.

79. Vocabulary for effect: synonyms

1 For example:
Students: pupils, exam candidates, learners
Improve: develop, enhance, extend
Learning: achievement, attainment, skills
Doing: completing, achieving, carrying out, performing

2 For example:

embarrassed	upset	scream	moment	annoyed
Answers provided on page 79 of Workbook	concerned worried alarmed	yell shriek shout	occasion time situation	aggravated agitated distressed

3 Answers will vary but all should include some of the synonyms from Question 2. For example:
On that day, on that occasion, I was mortified. I could have yelled or shouted, agitated as I was, but my sense of humiliation was total. I could barely manage a whisper. I tried to speak. Nothing. Alarmed at what they might be thinking, I took a deep breath and tried again.

80. Vocabulary for effect: creative

1 For example: Beams of sunlight danced on my walls.
2 The original sentence is over-written. It contains far too much description. Selecting vocabulary carefully is far more effective than cramming in as much description as possible.
3 Responses may include references to the visual impact of a place as well as the emotional impact. For example: Tenerife wasn't just a place to enjoy the seductive charm of the locals, the fervent power of the nightlife and the idyllic landscape – it was a place of refuge and escapism – the breath-taking volcanoes protected me from the sun's incessant glare, leaving me with a sense of claustrophobic wonder.
4 Answers could make reference to the contrived nature of the description; introducing emotional feelings would enable the writing to come alive for the reader. An improved answer could include alliteration ('tumultuous Tenerife'), a personal anecdote or a short sentence to vary the expression.
5 Answers will vary depending on words chosen.

81. Vocabulary for effect: viewpoint

1 For example:

A – Answer provided on page 81 of Workbook

B – 'use too many' could be replaced by: devour, fritter away; 'not have enough food' could be replaced by: starve

C – 'filled with' could be replaced by: dominated by, ruled by; 'not like' could be replaced by: hate, detest; 'cannot do much about it' could be replaced by: are powerless to change it

2 (a) For example: The word 'roar' suggests a lion and has connotations of loudness, anger, aggression and dominance. This would suggest that some parents are determined to fight the plans and win.

(b) For example: The word 'howl' suggests loudness, though perhaps a loudness that is ineffective, which creates the impression that the parents are protesting but that the plans will go ahead.

(c) For example: The word 'whimper' suggests weakness and that the parents do not present a real opposition to the school's plans.

3 Answers will vary but all should consist of two sentences and include vocabulary chosen for its impact and connotations. For example:

There are those who feel that people join the army in order to make a show of their bravery and to escape the monotonous drudgery of working 9–5 or other commitments to their family and society. Yet, these soldiers make a great sacrifice to protect us, many return severely injured and thousands receive no public recognition for their services but instead remain forlorn and forgotten.

82. Language for different effects 1

1 Extract A – Answer provided on page 82 of Workbook

Extract B – contrast, list, repetition

Extract C – contrast, list

Extract D – contrast

Extract E – contrast, rhetorical question

Extract F – repetition

2 Answers will vary but all should consist of four short extracts. Each extract should use one or more of the language techniques explored in Question 1. For example:

Contrast: Young new drivers are often over-confident, in spite of the fact that they are unpractised and uncertain in many of the traffic situations they find themselves in.

Repetition: We let 18-year-olds buy cigarettes. We let 18-year-olds buy alcohol. We let 18-year-olds vote. Young people should not have to wait until they are 21 to take their driving test.

Rhetorical question: Why has it taken so long for us to consider this crucial proposal?

List: At 17, teenagers are simply too immature, irresponsible, self-centred and impulsive to be allowed behind the wheel of a car.

83. Language for different effects 2

1 Extract A – hyperbole, alliteration

Extract B – direct address (and a rhetorical question)

Extract C – alliteration, pattern of three

Extract D – hyperbole

Extract E – pattern of three

Extract F – direct address

2 Answers will vary but all should consist of four short extracts. Each extract should use one or more of the language techniques explored in Question 1. For example:

Direct address: Do you really believe that our schools, the centres of learning that open for us so many doors of opportunity and of possibility, can be considered cruel?

Pattern of three: School is vital in teaching us to ask questions, seek answers and use our understanding to make the world a better place.

Alliteration: The cruelty of our crusty and crumbling school regime is designed to cripple the imagination and crush the soul.

Hyperbole: School is undoubtedly the cruellest and most confining form of imprisonment and torture found in the world today.

84. Language for different effects 3

1 Extract A – personification

Extract B – metaphor

Extract C – simile

Extract D – Answer provided on page 84 of Workbook

Extract E – metaphor

Extract F – personification

2 Answers will vary but all should consist of four short extracts. Each extract should use one of the figurative devices explored in Question 1. For example:

Simile: It is as clear as a recently cleaned window that the best way to engage students in their learning is to get on with the day as early as possible.

Metaphor: The current early start to the school day is the weight around the ankles of all those of us who are not naturally early risers.

Personification: The longer students are given in the morning, the longer their duvets will pin them down and prevent them from getting up at all.

Simile and personification: Teenagers are as sleepy as dormice and, ring as it might, an alarm clock frequently lacks the strength to drag them out of their slumber by itself.

85. Putting it into practice

1 Answers should include:
- language appropriate to the audience
- ambitious and effective language choices
- a range of language techniques, including figurative devices
- a consistent narrative voice.

86. Putting it into practice

1 Answers should include examples of:
- language appropriate to form, audience and purpose
- language chosen for effect
- figurative devices
- language techniques, e.g. rhetorical questions, patterns of three, etc.

87. Sentence variety 1

1 (a) B (multi-clause sentence with subordinate clause); it has two clauses, one of which is subordinate, linked with *because*

(b) E (minor sentence); it has no verb

(c) C (multi-clause sentence with coordinate clause); it has an equal pair of clauses, linked with *but*

(d) A (single-clause sentence). Answer provided on page 87

(e) D (multi-clause sentence with relative clause); the clause introduced by the relative pronoun *which* is separated from the main clause with commas

2 For example: Professional footballers are possibly the worst 'fakers'. With just one tap from another player they fall over, dive to the ground or occasionally fly. They always start screaming because it shows they are seriously injured. They say it was a foul. They demand a free kick. Ridiculous.

88. Sentence variety 2

1 For example:

(a) A pronoun – Answer provided on page 88 of Workbook

(b) An article – The big city with its bright lights and busy sounds is without a doubt the place for me.

(c) A preposition – Between the closely stacked tower blocks, you can just make out the occasional grey of the Thames.

(d) An -ing word (or present participle) – Crawling around the congested ring road in the sultry summer heat, I dream of country air and open spaces.

(e) An adjective – Slow is not a word for the big city, where speed is everything.

(f) An adverb – Happily, my flat is down a quiet side road and so the sounds of the city are subdued.

(g) A conjunction – Although I spent my childhood on a farm, city life suits me surprisingly well.

2 Answers will vary but all should aim to:
• include all seven different types of sentence opener from Question 1
• use a different word to start each sentence.
For example: **I** grew up in a tiny village in the middle of nowhere. **Although**, after such quiet beginnings, I was attracted by the hustle and bustle of city life, I know now that my heart belongs in the country. **The** city, with its bright lights and busy sounds, is suffocating to me. **Between** the closely stacked tower blocks, I peer in vain for a glimpse of the river and the hills, and only occasionally am I rewarded. **Walking** home after work last night, I raised my head to the stars of the winter sky and imagined myself at home, where the only hurry is in the current of the stream that runs through our meadow. **Slow** is not a word for the big city. **Unexpectedly**, however, as I raised my head, something wonderful happened.

89. Sentences for different effects

1 The effect of the long sentence is that it emphasises the chain of events, and builds tension as the situation worsens.
The effect of the short sentence is that it brings the scene to an abrupt end, focusing on the narrator's horror.

2 Sentence A – emphasises 'her' unsympathetic reaction
Sentence B – emphasises the long walk home
Note that the information the writer wants to emphasise usually comes at the end of the sentence.

3 Answers will vary but all should aim to include a:
• long sentence followed by a short sentence
• sentence structured to give specific emphasis.
For example: People and communities all over the world benefit from the money given to charities. Charities need our support.

90. Putting it into practice

1 Answers should include examples of:
• a range of sentence types
• sentences beginning in a range of different ways
• sentences structured for effect.

91. Ending a sentence

1 At the end of a sentence

2 At the end of a question

3 (a) Answer provided on page 91 of Workbook
(b) Avoid using them for anything other than an exclamation.
(c) Avoid using two or more exclamation marks in a row.

4 Sentence A is incorrect. This is a comma splice: two sentences are joined with a comma and they should be separated with a full stop or joined with a conjunction.
Sentence B is correct. The two sentences are separated with a full stop.
Sentence C is correct. The two sentences are joined with a conjunction.

5 There are eight mistakes in total in the original, including the unnecessary exclamation marks at the end of the title:
<u>A Change of Heart</u> [1]
I braced myself for a confrontation. [2] *She was looking at me like she knew I had something to say and she didn't want to hear it. My heart began to race and a strange throbbing pain pulsed in my forehead. How could I say it?* [3] *How could I tell her what I was thinking without upsetting her?* [4] *She knew something was coming.* [5] *Tears were welling up in her dark brown eyes and her bottom lip was starting to quiver. I didn't feel much better than she did.* [6] *My stomach was churning and I could feel my legs shaking. I tried to speak.* [7] *My mouth felt like sandpaper.* [8] *It was dry and rough and I couldn't form the words.*

92. Commas

1–2 A Incorrect: They can comfort us in a crisis, **[comma needed here]** help out when we're in trouble, **[comma needed here]** make us laugh or make us cry.
B Correct
C Correct
D Answer given on page 92 of Workbook
E Correct
F Incorrect: Although I had known her since primary school, **[comma needed here]** we never spoke again.
G Incorrect: The problem, **[comma needed here]** which we may not want to face, is that friends can sometimes let us down.
H Incorrect: A friend, **[comma needed here]** who I will not name, **[comma needed here]** once told me all my worst faults.
I Correct

3 Answers will vary but all should aim to use commas correctly to separate:
• items in a list
• a main and subordinate clause
• a main and relative clause.
For example: When I think back, I know that Alice was the perfect friend. Funny, clever, unswervingly loyal and eminently talented, Alice was also one of the kindest people I have ever known. One day, I admired, with considerable feelings of envy, her violin. Without a moment of hesitation, Alice passed me the instrument, which was a valuable family heirloom, and encouraged me to try it out.

93. Apostrophes and speech punctuation

1–2 A – Incorrect: should be *don't*
B – Correct
C – Incorrect: should be *wouldn't*
D – Incorrect: should be *teacher's* because it is singular (one teacher)
E – Correct

F – Correct (plural: several boys' faces)
G – Correct
H – Correct
I – Incorrect: 'Come over here, **|comma needed here|**' he whispered.

3 Answers will vary but all should aim to use apostrophes and speech marks correctly. For example:
'Hey,' she called. 'Come over here.'
'What do you want?' I asked, **full of curiosity.**
'Have you heard about Adam?'
'No, nothing. What about him?'
'Keep your voice down!' she hissed, 'People will hear.'
'Hear what exactly?' I whispered, beginning to feel a little impatient.
'Well, you know what he's been like lately. Apparently, more than one teacher has phoned his parents to complain.'
'I'm not surprised,' I said, wondering what all the fuss was about.

94. Colons, semi-colons, dashes, brackets and ellipses

1 For example:
A – There is only one thing you can do to improve your grades**: |colon, followed by lower case r for revise|** revise.
B – Teachers can help**: |colon, followed by lower case t for they|** they can give revision tips and answer any questions you have about the exam.
C – Revision isn't easy**: |colon, followed by lower case i for it|** it takes time and willpower.
D – Exams are the problem**; |semi-colon, followed by lower case r for revision|** revision is the solution.

2–3 A – Correct
B – Correct
C – Incorrect: *My bedroom walls are covered in scribbled revision notes and key points – not a pretty sight.* (Brackets **must** be used in pairs; dashes can be used singly.)
D – Answer given on page 94 of Workbook

4 Answers will vary but all should aim to use:
• a colon and a semi-colon
• dashes, brackets and an ellipsis.
For example: Deep breathing, positive mantras and assertive body language: this was Day One of the new me. I had never been a very confident person; I often struggled to believe in myself and in my own abilities. Yet, for a long time, it had been clear to me that something needed to change – and to change for the better. Many of my friends encouraged me, urging me on with warm words of support, while others (including my own mother) doubted I had the willpower to turn the corner. As I started to put the plans in place, I wondered who would turn out to be right…

95. Putting it into practice

1 Answers should feature a range of punctuation used accurately, including advanced punctuation, such as colons and semi-colons.

96. Common spelling errors 1

1 Sentence A – *their* (not *there*)
Sentence B – *would have* (not *would of*); *absolutely* (not *absolutley*)
Sentence C – *effect* (not *affect*); *extremely* (not *extremley*)
Sentence D – Correct
Sentence E – *There are* (not *Their our*)
Sentence F – *They're* (not *There*)
Sentence G – *its* (not *it's*)
Sentence H – *definitely* have (not *definitley* of)

Sentence I – *It's* (not *Its*); *are affected* (not *our effected*)
Sentence J – *our* (not *are*)
Sentence K – *could not have been* (not *could not of been*); *their* (not *there*)
Sentence L – *negatively* (not *negativley*)
Sentence M – *It's* (not *Its*)

97. Common spelling errors 2

1 Sentence A – *where* (not *were*); *whose* (not *who's*)
Sentence B – *Too* (not *To*)
Sentence C – *passed* (not *past*)
Sentence D – *pressure off us* (not *pressure of us*)
Sentence E – *You're* (not *Your*)
Sentence F – *Who's* (not *Whose*)
Sentence G – *were* (not *where*)
Sentence H – *past* (not *passed*); *were* (not *wear*)
Sentence I – *to an extreme* (not *too an extreme*)
Sentence J – Correct
Sentence K – *you're* (not *your*)
Sentence L – *off* (not *of*)
Sentence M – *we're* (not *were*)

98. Common spelling errors 3

1
argument	conscious
difficult	conscience
disappoint	experience
disappear	independence
embarrassing	believe
possession	weird
beginning	business
recommend	rhythm
occasionally	decision
definitely	grateful
separately	

2 Spelling practised will vary depending on the errors found in Question 1.

99. Proofreading

1 The corrections are shown in **bold**.
Scotland is the most amazing place **I've** ever visite**d. Even** though it took ten hours to drive **there,** it was worth it the moment **I** saw **where** we were staying: huge blue lochs, rolling green hills, miles and miles of pine forest. They even looked beautiful driving **past** them in a car.
On the first **day,** we took the dogs for a long walk through a forest. **It** was the **quietest** place **I've** ever been. Even with my brother **there**, all you could hear was the sound of **leaves** rustling in the breeze, the birds singing and **your** heart beating.
Our hotel was great**;** the **Scottish** people are so **friendly**. I would **definitely** stay there again.

2 Answers will vary depending on the work chosen.

3 Spelling practised will vary depending on the errors found in Question 2.

100. Putting it into practice

1 Answers should feature accurately used spelling, punctuation and grammar, and possibly signs of going back through the answer in order to make corrections.

Published by Pearson Education Limited, 80 Strand, London, WC2R 0RL.

www.pearsonschoolsandfecolleges.co.uk

Text © Pearson Education Limited 2016
Typeset by Kamae Design, Oxford
Produced by Out of House Publishing
Original illustrations © Pearson Education Limited 2016
Illustrated by Tech-Set Ltd, Gateshead
Cover illustration by Miriam Sturdee

The rights of Jonathan Morgan, Julie Hughes and David Grant to be identified as authors of this work have been asserted by them in accordance with the Copyright, Designs and Patents Act 1988.

First published 2016

18 17 16
10 9 8 7 6 5 4 3 2 1

British Library Cataloguing in Publication Data
A catalogue record for this book is available from the British Library

ISBN 9781447987833

Printed in Slovakia by Neografia

Acknowledgements

The publisher would like to thank the following for their kind permission to reproduce their photographs:

(Key: b-bottom; c-centre; l-left; r-right; t-top)

123RF.com: 65; **Getty Images**: VisitBritain / Jon Spaull 68; **Press Association Images**: Sport and General / S&G and Barratts / EMPICS Sport 95; **Shutterstock.com**: Fedor Selivanov 51, Specta 59, Vlue 115

All other images © Pearson Education

We are grateful to the following for permission to reproduce copyright material:

Text

Extract on page 101 from *A Day in the Life of Ivan Denisovich*, Orion Publishing Group (Solzhenitsyn A); Extract on page 102 Excerpt(s) from ENDURING LOVE by Ian McEwan, copyright © 1997 by Ian McEwan. Used by permission of Doubleday, an imprint of the Knopf Doubleday Publishing Group, a division of Penguin Random House LLC; Extract on page 103 from *To Kill a Mockingbird*, Arrow Books (Lee H) Penguin Random House and HarperCollins US; Extract on page 104 from *The Day of the Triffids*, Viking Books (Wyndham J) David Higham; Extract on page 106 from 'OK, you try teaching 13-year-olds', *The Guardian* (Hanson M) The Guardian; Extract on page 107 Excerpt(s) from THE BOYS ARE BACK by Simon Carr, copyright © 2000 by Simon Carr. Used by permission of Vintage Books, an imprint of the Knopf Doubleday Publishing Group, division of Penguin Random House LLC. All rights reserved; Extract on page 109 from ''Appy Ever After, *The Sunday Times*, 30/11/2014 (Arlidge J) News UK; Extract on page 111–113 from *I'm the King of the Castle*, Longman (Hill S) Sheil Land Associates Ltd; Extract on page 119 from 'The extraordinary story behind Danny Boyle's 127 Hours', *The Guardian*,15/12/2010 (Barkham P) The Guardian.

Note from the publisher

Pearson has robust editorial processes, including answer and fact checks, to ensure the accuracy of the content in this publication, and every effort is made to ensure this publication is free of errors. We are, however, only human, and occasionally errors do occur. Pearson is not liable for any misunderstandings that arise as a result of errors in this publication, but it is our priority to ensure that the content is accurate. If you spot an error, please do contact us at resourcescorrections@pearson.com so we can make sure it is corrected.

Printed in Great Britain
by Amazon

63971069R00079